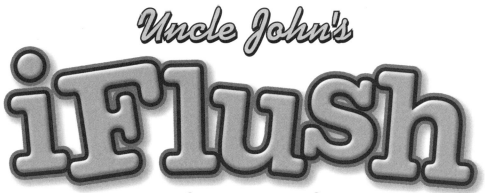

Uncle John's

iFlush

Swimming in Science

BATHROOM READER FOR KIDS ONLY!

ASPARAGUS-FREE ZONE

by
Patrick Merrell

Bathroom Readers' Press
Ashland, Oregon

UNCLE JOHN'S IFLUSH: SWIMMING IN SCIENCE
BATHROOM READER® FOR KIDS ONLY

For information, write:
The Bathroom Readers' Institute
P.O. Box 1117
Ashland, OR 97520
www.bathroomreader.com

Book design and illustration by Patrick Merrell

Dedicated to the Westchester Library System

ISBN-10: 1-60710-783-X / ISBN-13: 978-1-60710-783-5

Library of Congress Cataloging-in-Publication Data
Uncle John's iFlush swimming in science bathroom reader for kids only.
    pages cm
ISBN 978-1-60710-783-5 (hard cover)
1. Science–Miscellanea–Juvenile literature. 2. Curiosities and
wonders–Juvenile literature. I. Bathroom Readers' Institute (Ashland, Or.)
Q163.U53 2013
500–dc23

2012049150

Printed in the United States of America
First Printing: February, 2013

17 16 15 14 13   6 5 4 3 2 1

iOpener
Greetings

Prepare yourself for something you may have never thought possible. You're going to read about **science**… and love it! And I mean LOVE!

That is, unless you already love science. In which case, feel free to show this book to your friends and use your best "I told you so!" smirk. See, you were right all along: science rocks!

Here's just a **sampling** of what you'll find in the pages that follow:

- **Inventions:** an earthquake machine and a leech barometer.
- **Fabulous firsts:** a French rat in space and a 6-mile journey underwater.
- **Amazing animals:** a croc-eating snake and ocean-going rubber duckies.
- **Remarkable people:** The Birdman of India and a teenage fossil hunter.
- **Discoveries:** Pluto, the sometime planet, and acid-dripping snottites.

So, whenever you're ready, go to the…

Intro on page 6

And we're off and flushing!

Thanks!

A hearty high-four (sorry, that's all the fingers I have) to some humans who helped make this book possible:

Gordon Javna   Jay Newman   J. Carroll
Kim T. Griswell   Trina Janssen   Joan Kyzer
Brian Boone   Aaron Guzman   Erin Corbin
                    Blake Mitchum   Thomas Crapper

Contents

Bathroom user...

… prepare to dive into the greatest **toilet-themed adventure** ever devised by a group of **mad-scientist-type plumbers** and hosted by a bedraggled-yet-charming **lab rat** named **Dwayne**. That's me.

But, first, a quick explanation.

Copying how **computers** have been connected together to form the **Internet**, a top-secret plumbing team known as the **Four P's** linked the world's **sewer lines** together to create the **Interpipe**. You probably think I'm making that up, but this book is based on how it actually works!

The Four P's

Plumb Bob
Phyllis Tanks
P. Liddy
Portia Potty

Flush yourself down a toilet in **Walla Walla** (that's a city in the northwest part of the United States) and next thing you know, you're in **Katmandu** (that's like all the way on the other side of the world).

Wait, it gets even better!

The Four P's also created a waterproof device called the **iSwirl** that can be used to travel back in time, spinning through the years in a mere flush of the toilet! Is that not totally cool…and wet?

Yeah, I thought you'd agree.

So here's how this is going to work.

I'm gonna flush myself down this toilet, and you're gonna follow along. I'll be visiting a **different place** and a **different year** every time you turn the page. Solve the **puzzle** you find there, and you can move on — in one of three ways.

1. Follow the **pipes** to the next page; **2.** jump to the page shown on the **iSwirl** (in the lower right-hand corner) — the "**jump route**" will take you through the book in **chronological order** (from the earliest date to the most recent); or **3.** visit pages any old way you want!

Sound like a plan?

Then let's get going! I'll jump in, you turn the page, and we're on our way!

Note:

If you want to keep your book clean, use a separate piece of paper (toilet paper not recommended!) for solving the puzzles.

2. Jump using the iSwirl

Go to the page shown.

1. Follow the pipes

700 B.C. Wow, we've traveled back nearly 3,000 years to a **royal palace** in **Assyria** where the mysterious **Nimrud Lens** was created!

It wasn't until 1850 that an English **archeologist** dug up the lens, which is now on display in a British museum that's called … get this … the **British Museum**! How'd they think that one up? :-)

The Nimrud Lens

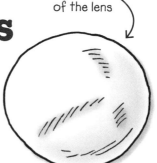

actual size of the lens

It's called a **lens**, but is that really what it is? People have been wondering about that for years.

Experts agree on two things: 1) the Nimrud Lens is made of rock crystal, and 2) it is thicker in the middle, just like a lens. But that's about it.

Some people think it was used to focus the **sun's rays** to start fires. Others think it was a **magnifying glass** Assyrian craftsmen used for making their detailed artwork.

One scientist claimed it was part of an **ancient telescope** (allowing the Assyrians to see snakes circling Saturn!). Others have suggested it's nothing more than a **decoration** for a piece of furniture.

I was hoping to get the answer from an **Assyrian girl** standing nearby, but when I started talking, she ran away. Weird. :-(So I guess we'll just have to go on asking, "What is the mysterious Nimrud Lens?"

Make a Lens Out of Water!

It's simple. Get a clear piece of plastic or glass and lay it on top of this page. Then put a tiny drop of water on it. Look at the type through the water. Because the water drop bulges up in the middle like a lens, the letters will be magnified. **Warning:** If your water drop is too big, it will flatten out and won't work.

The Assyrians were great artists, architects, astronomers, and fighters.

iPuzzle
Lens Sense

Each answer below is missing one L, one E, one N, and one S (in any order). Use the clues to help you complete each word.

1. Quickly, without warning: __ U D D __ __ __ Y

2. Sour yellow fruits: __ __ M O __ __

3. Use one's ears: __ I __ T __ __

4. Sharp tiny piece of wood: __ P __ I __ T __ R

5. Two-person sport on a mat: W R __ __ T __ I __ G

6. Like money a bankrobber takes: __ T O __ __ __

7. Fuel pumped into a car: G A __ O __ I __ __

8. Farthest from start to finish: __ O __ G __ __ T

9. Horns on top of a deer's head: A __ T __ __ R __

Don't know what this is? It's all explained on page 7.

Jump to this page **or** follow the pipes.

Know Your Lenses: Lenses are used in lots of things—telescopes, CD players, car headlights, apartment door peepholes, cameras, eyeglasses, and submarine periscopes.

A double-concave lens makes things look smaller. A double-convex lens can make things look bigger, smaller, or even upside-down depending on how far away it's held!

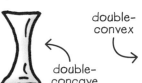

double-concave

double-convex

If it has one flat side, use "plano."

plano-concave

plano-convex

The lens is named after the lentil, a soup vegetable that's shaped like a double-convex lens.

1961

We're in the middle of the **Sahara Desert** with a **rat** who's just been shot into **space**. Yes, a rat!

Hector the Astro-Rat

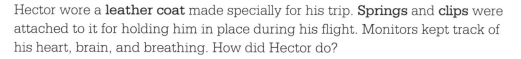

In the 1950s and 1960s, the **United States** and the **Soviet Union** were racing to be the first to put a person in space. But before they shot any humans up, they used animals to see if their rockets would work.

The United States started with **monkeys** (after a few tests with fruit flies). The Soviet Union used **dogs**, which they thought were better at sitting still in tight spaces.

Meanwhile, **France** was doing some rocket testing of its own. That country's first **astronaut**? A **white rat** named **Hector**. Yay, Hector! <:3( )~

Hector wore a **leather coat** made specially for his trip. **Springs** and **clips** were attached to it for holding him in place during his flight. Monitors kept track of his heart, brain, and breathing. How did Hector do?

Great! He traveled up 95 miles (152 km), sitting snugly in the **nose cone** of a **Véronique rocket**, which safely parachuted back to earth.

The test took place in Africa's huge **Sahara Desert** at the **Hammaguir** launch site in **French Algeria**. Why there? Well, for one thing — there are no houses or trees to land on!

Who Was Next?

A year after Hector, France sent up two rats named Castor and Pollux, and then two cats. A stray cat named Felix was going to be the first cat in space, but he ran away and had to be replaced by a girl cat named Felicette. Yay, Felix. Hee-hee.

An English ice-cream company featured Hector on one of its collectible "Space Exploration" cards in the 1960s.

iPuzzle
Space Zoo Search

Look for each name either forward, backward, up, down, or diagonally.

ALBERT
BELISARIO
CASTOR
DEZIK
ENOS
FELICETTE
FELIX
HAM
HECTOR
LAIKA
POLLUX
TSYGAN

```
I D A V C Y K M N Q S J
F E R C K M Y H T O R X
P Z M Z U H A M N Z O I
O I R A S I L E B E T L
L K T B E S B A X K C E
L X X E T T E C I L E F
U C A S T O R N J K H J
X Y U H B C T S Y G A N
```

Space Zoo: Some animal astronauts over the years.

1947: fruit flies (U.S.)
1949: Albert II the monkey (U.S.)
1951: Tsygan and Dezik, female dogs (U.S.S.R.)
1957: Laika the dog, first animal to orbit Earth (U.S.S.R.)
1959: monkeys Able and Baker (U.S.)
1961: Ham, first chimp in space (U.S.)
1961: Hector the rat (France)
1961: Enos, first chimp to orbit Earth (U.S.)
1963: Felicette the cat (France)
1964: white mice (China)
1967: Belisario the rat (Argentina)

Also: rabbits, hamsters, guinea pigs, spiders, ants, bees, wasps, newts, snails, frogs, turtles, tortoises, jellyfish, shrimp, fish, sea urchins, and Mexican jumping beans.

Jump to this page **or** follow the pipes.

A puppy from the Soviet space dog Strelka was given to President Kennedy's daughter, Caroline.

Dead end.

1898

We've arrived at **Nikola Tesla's lab** in downtown **Manhattan** just a few minutes *after* he tested his so-called...

Earthquake Machine

Nikola Tesla was one of the greatest **inventors** of all time. **Thomas Edison**, who lived at the same time, is more famous today. That's because he was a better **businessman**, hiring a team of talented **scientists** that cranked out new or improved products. But Tesla came up with tons of new **ideas** and **inventions** that left others scratching their heads.

Not all of his ideas worked out. Some even sounded a little crazy, like sending an **electric current** high into the air to make the sky glow at night. Could that really work? Who knows? Before Tesla had a chance to try it out, his mind was working on something else.

Back to Tesla's **earthquake machine**: The idea is pretty simple. An object will shake when vibrated. But if the right **vibration rate** is used, it will shake a lot. Kinda like pushing a **swing**. If you push at just the right moments, the swing will go higher.

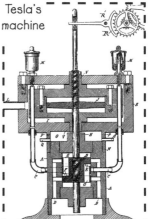

Tesla's machine

Tesla's earthquake machine used that idea. And, from what he says, it worked so well his whole **neighborhood** started shaking! First a **metal post** in his lab, then the **building** his lab was in, then everything up and down the street.

People were running around in panic, and Tesla had to destroy the machine with a **sledgehammer** before it did any real damage. The **police** came rushing through the door of his lab just as he did.

Could this story possibly be true? No one has ever been able to do the same thing—or anything close to it. But, given all the amazing ideas Tesla dreamed up and proved true, I'm not the rat to say it didn't happen.

Tesla was a Serb born in what's now called Croatia. He became an American citizen at age 35.

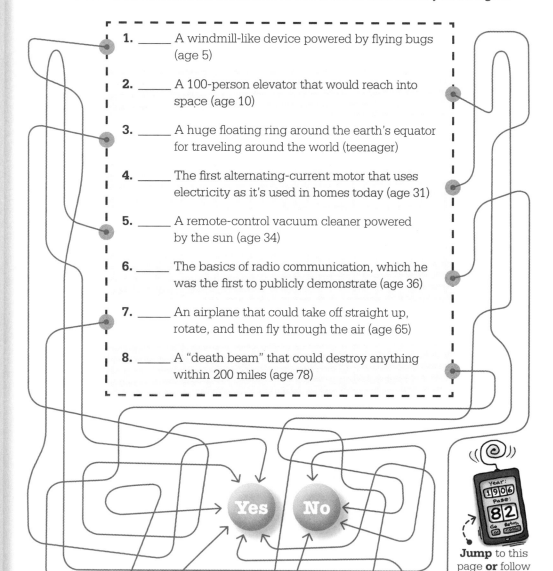

iPuzzle
Tesla: Yes or No?

Which of these ideas did Nikola Tesla come up with? Take a guess by writing YES or NO in each blank. Then follow the lines to find out if you're right.

1. _____ A windmill-like device powered by flying bugs (age 5)

2. _____ A 100-person elevator that would reach into space (age 10)

3. _____ A huge floating ring around the earth's equator for traveling around the world (teenager)

4. _____ The first alternating-current motor that uses electricity as it's used in homes today (age 31)

5. _____ A remote-control vacuum cleaner powered by the sun (age 34)

6. _____ The basics of radio communication, which he was the first to publicly demonstrate (age 36)

7. _____ An airplane that could take off straight up, rotate, and then fly through the air (age 65)

8. _____ A "death beam" that could destroy anything within 200 miles (age 78)

Yes   No

Jump to this page **or** follow the pipes.

Tesla could picture in his head exactly how an invention would work before it had been built.

Near the end of his life, Tesla wrote of falling in love with a white pigeon.

1794 Welcome to **France** and the workplace of **Nicolas-Jacques Conté**, the inventor of the **pencil** as we it know today.

Yes, you heard that right, the pencil! It's cheap, can be taken anywhere, and has tons of uses — sketching, writing grocery lists, solving puzzles. And, best of all, if you don't like what you see, you can just erase it!

French-Baked Pencils

The story of the pencil started in the 1560s when a mine of pure **graphite** was discovered in **Borrowdale, England**. Legend has it that **shepherds** found it when the roots of a fallen tree tore the ground open. They liked the smooth black lines it made so much that they started using chunks of it to mark their **sheep**.

The English called the stuff **plumbago**, which means "lead ore" in **Latin.** (It was centuries before people figured out it was graphite, not lead.)

Small pieces of plumbago, wrapped in **string** or held in **hollow tubes**, were soon being used all across the world. People couldn't get enough of it, and England had the only known pure supply.

Two hundred years later, that was still the case, which was a problem for the French. They were at **war** with England and couldn't get any plumbago. How were French **schoolkids** supposed to take their tests?!

The French **Minister of War** decided to do something about it and asked **Nicolas-Jacques Conté**, an engineer and inventor, if he could come up with something. It wasn't long before Conté had the answer.

There were other places to get graphite. But it wasn't pure. It had to be crushed into a powder to get rid of the impurities. So Conté used **graphite powder** instead, mixed it with **potter's clay** and **water**, and baked thin sticks of it at high heat. Two pieces of **wood** were then glued around each baked stick.

And that's the way that pencils are still made today!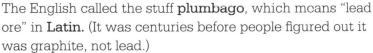

Graphite is a form of carbon. So are diamonds.

Conté was a successful portrait painter at the age of 14.

iPuzzle
One-Line Drawings

Can you draw each of the figures below in one
continuous line? You can't lift your pencil off the paper
or retrace any part of the line you've already drawn.

EXAMPLE:

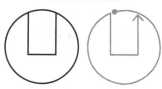

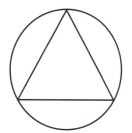

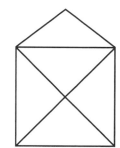

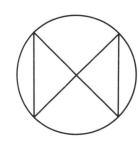

Impossible Trick: Draw a dot and a
circle without lifting your pencil off the paper!

1. Draw a dot
in the middle
of your paper.

2. Fold the top
of the paper
down to just
above the
dot (use your
other hand).

3. Draw up
onto the
folded part,
over to the
side, and
then back
down off the
folded part.

1.

2.

3.

4.

4. Unfold the flap and draw the
circle. Your pencil never left the
paper!

Jump to this
page **or** follow
the pipes.

Erasers were first added to the ends of pencils in 1858.

1972 Video games have been around your whole life (unless you're some **geezer** sneaking a peek at this book). But 40 years ago, kids didn't have such things. That all changed one day with a game called ...

Pong

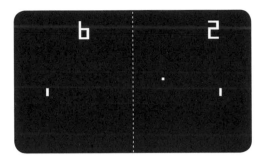

Pong wasn't the first video game, but it was the first one played by more than a few people in some computer geek's **workroom**. Millions of people played it all across the United States.

It was incredibly simple compared to today's full-color 3-D games. It was just a **black screen** with two rectangles that hit a square ball back and forth across a dotted-line net. The only **instructions** were, "Avoid missing ball for high score." Wow! Who wrote that masterpiece?

Atari, the maker of the game, wasn't much of a company at the time. It was just a few people in a small office of a concrete building. One employee, **Al Alcorn**, was given the job of creating an electronic **ping-pong game**, but even his bosses didn't think much would come of it.

Alcorn made two smart decisions. First, he designed the **paddle** so it could hit the ball in different directions. That added more skill to the game. The center of the paddle hit the ball straight across the screen. The top or bottom parts hit it at an angle, and the very edges hit it at an even sharper angle. Second, Alcorn programmed the game so that the longer it took to score a point, the faster the ball moved.

How did the game do? The first machine was put on top of a **barrel** in the back room of a **bar** near Atari's office, and it soon stopped working—because it was overstuffed with **quarters** from people playing it so much!

Atari started making games as fast as they could. Pong quickly became the most popular **arcade game** in America.

Alcorn's test version of Pong used a $75 black-and-white TV to display the game.

iPuzzle
Maze Ball

Avoid the holes and get the ball from START to END.

NEW!
From iFlush
Labs

As seen
on radio!

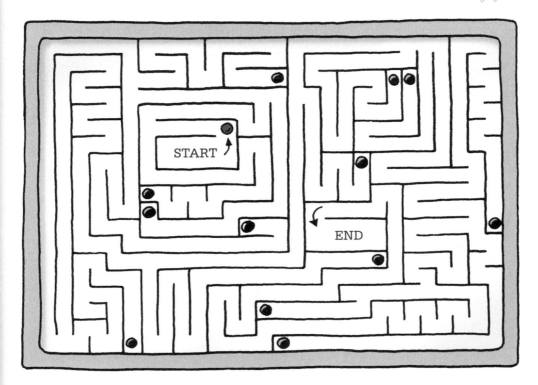

START

END

Pong's Song: One of Al Alcorn's bosses wanted him to add the sound of a cheering crowd at the end of each point. His other boss wanted boos and hisses. But Al didn't know how to create any of those sounds, and he didn't have enough parts anyway.

Instead, he found noises that his game could already make and ended up with a few electronic bloops and bleeps. Some thought it was the perfect choice, but the truth is it was just the easiest way Al could find to do it.

BLIP
BLUZZLE
BLEEP
BLOOP

Year:
1973
Page:
36
Go Return

Jump to this page **or** follow the pipes.

1732 We're in **Bologna, Italy**, where 20-year-old **Laura Bassi** has just been made a **University of Bologna** professor.

Professor Bassi

So what's the big deal? People become **professors** all the time, right? Well, back then in **Europe**, women didn't. **Laura Bassi** was the first.

In Bologna in the early 1700s some people thought the idea of women studying at **universities** was a good idea. But the only women to come close to getting in were from powerful families trying to make it happen for their own daughters. It didn't. That all changed when Laura Bassi came along.

Laura, a lawyer's daughter, was smart. Really smart. At age five, she started studying math, French, and Latin; and she learned quickly. Her family's doctor, **Gaetano Tacconi**, was so impressed that, when Laura was 13, he agreed to tutor her (he was also a university teacher).

For the next seven years, Dr. Tacconi taught Laura the subjects offered at the universities she couldn't attend. Things like **science** and **logic** and **philosophy**. This was supposed to be a secret, but the word spread and visitors were soon stopping by the house to meet this bright girl.

In 1732, Dr. Tacconi arranged to have a group of professors from the University of Bologna test Bassi. Passing would make her a university **graduate**. All of Bologna heard what was going on and wanted to witness the event. The usually private test was moved to the **city's palace** to handle the crowds.

On the day of the event, Bassi arrived in a **carriage** and took her place in a hall packed with officials, royalty, and curious onlookers. She answered questions on **49 topics** and nailed it, sometimes to applause. A month later, in a huge celebration (poems were even written about her!), she got her **university degree**. She'd graduated.

That fall, after passing one final test, Laura Bassi became Europe's first female professor. In December 1732, she gave her first **lecture** in the main building of the University of Bologna.

In the 1760s, Bassi focused on experiments with electricity, a mostly unknown field then.

iPuzzle
Bronze Medal

A medal was made to honor Laura Bassi in 1732. Which five pieces below can be put together to make a complete medal?

Shown at 80% of actual size

1.

2.

3.

4.

5.

6.

7.

8.

9.

The Rest of Her Life: Laura Bassi went on to have a long career in science, on top of having eight children. For 28 years, she taught physics in her home, paid for by the university. She was one of the main people to bring the new ideas of Isaac Newton to Italy (he's the guy who "discovered" gravity). Other important honors and posts followed. Bassi died in 1778 at the age of 66.

Year: 1776 Page: 60

Jump to this page **or** follow the pipes.

1939

I've made my way to the **1939 New York World's Fair** to get a look at ...

Elektro, the Moto-Man

Elektro was a 7-foot-tall, 260-pound **robot** built by **Westinghouse** to show what the **household helper** of the future might look like. I guess they figured people were gonna need a walking tin can that could wiggle its fingers, flash a pair of light-bulb eyes, and repeat jokes using a record player. Maybe not ... but that didn't stop over 3 million people from lining up so see him do all those things.

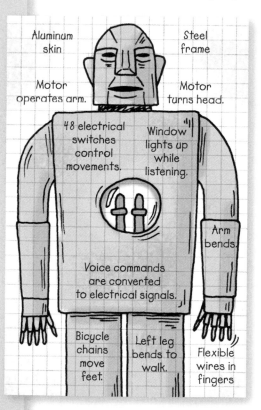

- Aluminum skin
- Steel frame
- Motor operates arm.
- Motor turns head.
- 48 electrical switches control movements.
- Window lights up while listening.
- Arm bends.
- Voice commands are converted to electrical signals.
- Bicycle chains move feet.
- Left leg bends to walk.
- Flexible wires in fingers

Commands were given by talking slowly into a **telephone**. Elektro didn't actually understand the words. The number of spoken sounds triggered his responses. Among his answers: "My brain is bigger than yours" or "If you use me well, I can be your slave."

After the fair, Elektro toured the country in a **bread truck** and then became an amusement park attraction at the **Pacific Ocean Park** in California. He also appeared in some ads.

He was then taken apart and forgotten. Years later, the son of one of his builders hunted down all his parts (his head was in someone's basement) and put Elektro back together. He now stands proudly in the **Mansfield Memorial Museum** in Ohio.

Elektro's Voice

Elektro was filled with gears, switches, pulleys, rubber rollers for walking, and even a bellows for blowing up balloons. But his voice came from record players offstage, which received signals from switches inside Elektro.

Westinghouse buried a time capsule (filled with common 1939 items) at the World's Fair, not to be opened for 5,000 years.

iPuzzle
Robot Code

Use this key to figure out the answers to both jokes.

▲	🔩	★	🌙	🏠	✏️	⚡	🔧	🔌	💧	☀️	▱
A	E	H	L	M	R	S	T	U	V	W	Y

What is Elektro's favorite kind of music?

Why did Elektro have to go back to robot school?

EXTRA CREDIT: Computers inside robots count in binary. That means they only use the numbers 0 and 1. Counting starts the same: 1 written in binary is 1, but 2 in binary is 10. If 3 is 11, 4 is 100, 5 is 101, and 6 is 110, what is 9 in binary?

- -

Elektro's Robot Relatives: Before Elektro, there were a number of other robots Westinghouse built, starting in 1927. They included:

Herbert Televox, Mr. Telelux, Katrina Van Televox, and Willie Vocalite. Willie could even fire a gun! Sparko, a robot dog that could bark, sit, and wag his tail, joined Elektro for one year at the World's Fair in 1940.

Jump to this page **or** follow the pipes.

The 1939 World's Fair had the futuristic theme "Dawn of a New Day."

1853 This stop might be the most important scientific breakthrough in this book. We're at **Moon's Lake House,** a restaurant in **Saratoga Springs**, New York, where the **potato chip** was invented.

What, you don't think the potato chip is an important scientific invention? Well, to me and my rat friends, it's right up there at the top of the garbage heap! Maybe second only to leftover **pizza crusts**. Or **cheesy snacks**. Yum!

Chip, Chip, Hooray!

During the **summer**, people would flock to the natural **mineral springs** found all around this area. And many of them would stop by Moon's Lake House to enjoy a tasty evening meal on the shores of **Saratoga Lake**.

George Crum, a chef at the restaurant, liked to boast he could make a great meal out of just about anything. And most everyone agreed. But once in a while, a **diner** would dare to complain about something Crum served. They'd soon be sorry they did. Crum was one ornery fellow, and he'd send out something to replace the item that was much, much worse! He'd then peek out the kitchen door to see the shocked reaction ... and smile. Hee-hee. :-)

Well, one day, a diner sent back an order of the restaurant's famous **french-fried potatoes**. He thought they were too large and soggy. As usual, Crum was not at all happy, and he quickly set to work to make the world's worst french fries. He sliced up a **potato** as thin as possible and threw the pieces in a pot of **boiling grease**. They were then salted and sent out to the complainer.

crunch munch

An odd thing happened. As Crum watched from the door, he saw the man gobble them down—and then order more. Other diners were curious and wanted to try them as well. Crum's fried creation, which the restaurant soon named **Saratoga chips**, was a big hit.

Word spread, and people all across the United States and the world have been enjoying potato chips ever since.

George Crum was born George Speck but took the name his father used as a jockey ...turning a Speck into a Crum!

George Crum's mother was a Huron Indian and his father an African American.

iPuzzle
Spud Jokes

Which punch line goes with which joke? Write the letters in the blanks.

1. ___ Why did the potato cross the road?

2. ___ What do you call a potato that goes to football games?

3. ___ How do you make a potato laugh?

4. ___ Why was the potato chip all alone at the party?

5. ___ How do you get a baked potato to do what you want?

6. ___ What kind of potato makes a good detective?

7. ___ What do you get if you cross Santa and a potato?

8. ___ What do you call a man in a monastery who eats fried-potato snacks?

9. ___ Where are dead potatoes buried?

10. ___ What do you call a baby potato?

A. It got there oily.

B. One whose eyes are peeled.

C. A chip monk.

D. It saw a fork up ahead.

E. In gravy-yards.

F. A jolly man who says "Idaho-ho-ho."

G. Tickle its pota-toes.

H. Butter it up.

I. A spec-tater.

J. A small fry.

A couch potato on a potato couch

Hyperbolic Paraboloid

That's the mathematical name for the saddlelike shape of a potato chip. So impress people the next time you're eating some chips, and tell them you're consuming hyperbolic paraboloids!

Jump to this page **or** follow the pipes.

In 1926, Laura Scudder was the first to package potato chips in waxed-paper bags, which kept them fresh.

1851

We're at the **Great Exhibition** in London's **Crystal Palace**. It's where some of the great inventions of the day are on display. It's also where **Dr. George Merryweather** is showing off his not-so-great…

Leech Barometer

Dr. Merryweather dreamed of finding a better way to predict storms. Unfortunately, his dream involved **leeches**, those little sluglike creatures that live in **swamps**, stick themselves onto people's bodies, and suck blood. Let's all say it together—yeeuuck! :-(

A **barometer** is a device that helps predict the weather. It measures changes in the **air pressure** around you (air is actually heavy and presses down on you all the time). A simple barometer is nothing more than a **glass tube** filled with water, like the one I'm holding. If the water level drops quickly, that means low air pressure, and rain is probably on the way.

But that wasn't good enough for Dr. Merryweather (is that a perfect name, or what?). He found a way to make his barometer much more complicated. And expensive. And, uh, filled with leeches.

According to the good doctor, leeches had long been known to react to changes in air pressure. They'd get all excited in their swampy homes when a storm was on the way and the air pressure dropped. So, Merryweather thought, why not bottle these talented leeches?

He called his creation the **Tempest Prognosticator** (a fancy way of saying storm predictor), and here's how it worked: 12 bottles sat on a tray, each containing water, a leech, and a piece of **whale bone**. A string traveled from each whale bone to a bell at the top. When a storm approached, the air pressure dropped, 12 leeches started dancing about, and all those jiggling strings caused the bell to ring. Genius, right?

This fancy model used silver, brass, and mahogany wood.

Bell

The leeches went in these bottles.

Merryweather's leech barometer was designed to look like an Indian temple.

iPuzzle
On Display

Six of the items described below were displayed at the Great Exhibition of 1851. Two weren't. Here's how to find the fakes:

Solve the math problems in the box. Each answer will match the number of a real item. Check those off. The two items left unchecked are the fakes.

1. ___ A piano that could be played by four people at the same time

2. ___ A train engine powered by two sails and a windmill

3. ___ A sculpture of the queen of England made of soap

4. ___ Stuffed kittens propped up and dressed in clothes

5. ___ A 10-foot-tall trophy made of black rubber

6. ___ A double-decker bathtub made of gold

7. ___ A bed that could turn into a lifeboat

8. ✓ The world's largest diamond •------------------->

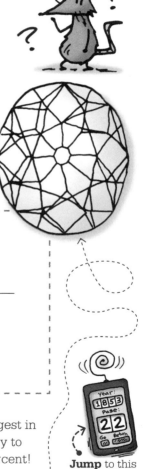

A. Days in a week + wheels on a unicycle = ___8___

B. Legs on an insect − legs on a bird = _____

C. Eyes a cyclops has + cell-phone key with GHI on it = _____

D. Stripes on the U.S. flag − a dozen = _____

E. Sides on a stop sign − arms on most starfish = _____

F. Seasons in the year + singers in a trio = _____

The Kohinoor diamond was the world's largest in
1851. A year later, England's Prince Albert had it recut to try to make it sparkle more. Doing that reduced its size by 42 percent! Even worse, he wasn't happy with how it turned out. The drawing above is how it looks now, actual size. •- - - - - -

Jump to this page **or** follow the pipes.

Year: 1853 Page: 22 Go Return

Merryweather placed the bottles next to each other in a circle so the leeches wouldn't feel lonely. Really! He said that.

An essay describing the leech barometer was presented to Queen Victoria, the queen of England at the time.

1973

Putting **soda** in a **plastic bottle** is no big deal, right? I mean, it doesn't take a genius to figure that one out.

In fact, it does! It took inventor **Nat Wyeth** six years of experimenting to find a way to do it.

Fizz Whiz

Nat Wyeth's father was the famous artist and illustrator **N.C. Wyeth**. His brother was the famous painter **Andrew Wyeth**. His three sisters—Henriette, Carolyn, and Ann—were well-known artists as well. So what did Nat become? No, not an artist—an **engineer** and **inventor**.

Nat Wyeth never wanted to be an artist. As a boy, when the rest of the family was drawing or painting, he would be taking apart watches or building gadgets. He once made a **toy speedboat** using, among other things, old watch parts.

Encouraged by his father, he studied **engineering** in college and ended up working for the **Du Pont** company in Delaware. Early projects included creating a cheap, plastic-like fabric called **Typar** and designing a machine for making sticks of **dynamite**.

But his most famous creation was the **plastic soda bottle**. In 1967, when he first started working on it, he'd heard plastic bottles couldn't hold soda. To see for himself, he bought a bottle of **washing machine soap**, emptied it, filled it with ginger ale, and left it in the **refrigerator** overnight. By the next morning, the bottle had swollen up so much he couldn't get it out of the refrigerator!

Wyeth realized he needed something stronger, something that could stand up to the **bubbles** inside. The solution was to: 1) use a different type of plastic and 2) stretch the plastic. Stretching forced the molecules in the plastic to line up, which made it stronger. But he had to find a way to stretch the plastic in both directions, so the bottle was strong up and down *and* side to side.

He did that by forcing a blob of plastic into a tube with a crisscrossing "screw thread" pattern. That stretched the plastic in both directions. The plastic was then blown up like a balloon inside a bottle-shaped mold. *Ta da*! The world had its first plastic soda bottle.

Wyeth felt mistakes were an important part of coming up with successful inventions.

Some of Wyeth's co-workers told him his idea of making a plastic soda bottle was impossible. That inspired him even more.

iPuzzle
Plastic Surgery

The plastic used in Wyeth's bottle is known as PET, which is short for polyethylene terephthalate. How's that for a mouthful?

We've cut those words up and rearranged the letters to form new words. As you fill in each blank, cross off the letters above. Every letter will be used.

POLYETHYLENE

1. Back part of a human foot: ____ ____ ____ ____

2. Use a computer keyboard to write words: ____ ____ ____ ____

3. iFlush is "For Kids ____ ____ ____ ____ !"

TEREPHTHALATE

4. Square of butter: ____ ____ ____

5. Shoes and belts are often made out of it: ____ ____ ____ ____ ____ ____ ____

6. The most common word in the English language: ____ ____ ____

POLYETHYLENE   TEREPHTHALATE

7. Not sick: ____ ____ ____ ____ ____ ____ ____

8. Big animal with a trunk: ____ ____ ____ ____ ____ ____ ____ ____

9. Snakelike fish: ____ ____ ____

10. Bowls and vases made of clay: ____ ____ ____ ____ ____ ____ ____

"Get off Route 25" That was inventor Charles Kettering's motto and one that Nat Wyeth often followed. It means don't keep going down the same road if a solution isn't coming. Try something new, come at the problem from a different direction.

Year: 1989 Page: 70 Go Return

Jump to this page **or** follow the pipes.

Dead end.
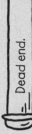

1999 We're in **England** in the office of **Eva Crane**, one of the all-time great **beekeeping** experts. Her masterpiece, *The World History of Beekeeping and Honey Hunting*, has just been published.

The Bee Queen

How does one become an expert on bees? Well, here's the Eva Crane method: 1) study **math** and **nuclear physics** in college, then 2) get married and have someone give you a box of bees as a wedding present. Why bees? Crane was married during **World War II**, when sugar was scarce. The bees could make honey for her.

Crane became bee-dazzled with her **hive** of little buzzers. She spent the next 50 years learning just about everything there was to know about beekeeping. She edited bee magazines, and she ran the **International Bee Research Association**, one of the world's great sources of beekeeping info.

Her work took her to 60 countries. She traveled by **dogsled** in Alaska (yes, there are bees in Alaska) and **dugout canoe** in Vietnam. She climbed cliffs in the Spanish **Pyrenees** mountains (at age 74) and flew over African plains.

In a village in northern India, she saw **mud houses** with hives built into their walls. Inside the houses, she was amazed to find **clay honey dishes** identical to ones dug up in ancient **Greek ruins** 2,800 miles away (4,500 km).

In the U.S., Crane visited the spot where the **Virginia colonists** first brought **honey bees** to America in the 1620s. In Mexico, she saw stacks of **log hives** much like the ones the ancient **Mayans** used. On the Caribbean island of Antigua, she discovered that hives were placed on high stands to keep them away from giant **bee-eating toads**. In Kenya, she watched as a secret recipe of **herbs** was rubbed on new hives to attract bees. In Australia, she saw **beeswax** that was used as glue by the native people.

It was as if Eva Crane were a bee herself, gathering knowledge from around the world, then coming back to her "hive" to turn it into papers, articles, books, and lectures, hundreds in all.

iPuzzle
Making a Beeline

Starting and ending at the hive, find a path that visits every flower just once without traveling along the same dotted line twice.

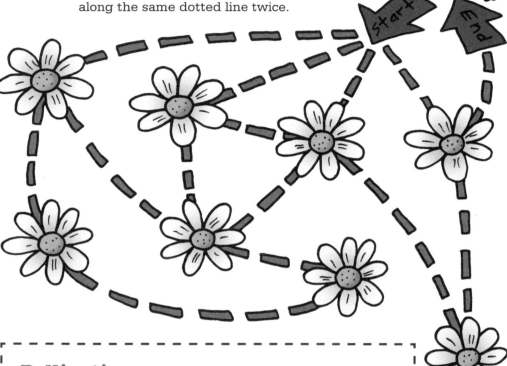

Pollination: Bees help create lots of the foods we love.
While collecting pollen to make their honey, bees move pollen from one plant to another, fertilizing it. Many tasty things are created that way. Here are some:

- fruits such as apples, cherries, and watermelons;
- nuts such as cashews, peanuts, and almonds;
- herbs such as basil, mustard, and caraway;
- vegetables such as carrots, celery, and peas;
- cotton, coffee, and cocoa;
- tea plants and…asparagus! (Hey, nobody's perfect!);
- plus flowers such as lilacs, petunias, and buttercups.

Jump to this page **or** follow the pipes.

1885

We're in the workplace of a man who had a big role in the creation of two really important inventions — the **telephone** and the **light bulb**.

Lewis Latimer

As a boy, **Lewis Latimer** was a good student who loved to read and draw. Those interests would help him become a big success later on.

Latimer's first job, in 1865, was as an office boy at a **Boston law firm** that helped inventors protect their **patents** (proof they were the original creators). He closely watched the **draftsmen** who made detailed drawings of each invention. And, after a lot of study and practice, he became an expert draftsman himself.

Latimer's work caught the eye of **Alexander Graham Bell**, who was busy creating the **telephone**. Bell hired him to make the drawings for his invention. They worked late into the night because Bell was racing against another inventor, **Elisha Gray**. On Valentine's Day in 1876, Bell filed his application with the patent office, just beating out Gray!

Latimer's abilities grew, and in 1881 he and another man patented a light bulb **filament** (the glowing part inside a bulb) made of **carbon**. It was an improvement over the one used by Thomas Edison in his new version of the light bulb.

Latimer was soon hired by Edison and became an incredibly valuable employee. He could draw inventions, he knew how they worked, he was an expert at getting and protecting patents, and he could oversee construction projects. He also translated French and German for Edison and ran the company's library.

- - - - - - - - - - - -

George Latimer, Lewis's Father

Lewis's father, George, grew up as a slave in Virginia. But in 1842, at the age of 23, he decided he'd had enough. He and his wife escaped to Massachusetts. He was arrested and was at the center of a big legal battle. Finally, a preacher paid $400 to buy George's freedom. But George had no papers to show he was a free man, and he lived the rest of his life worrying he'd be arrested again.

In 1864, at the age of 16, Lewis falsified his age and joined the U.S. Navy to fight in the Civil War.

Lewis Latimer also wrote plays and poetry, played the flute, and painted.

iPuzzle
In Other Words

How many words of three or more letters can you make using only the letters in LATIMER? Try to get a dozen words, but keep going if you can.

LATIMER

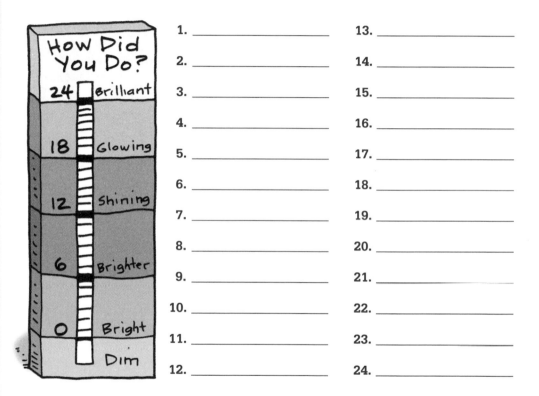

How Did You Do?

24 ☐ Brilliant
18 Glowing
12 Shining
6 Brighter
0 Bright
Dim

1. _____
2. _____
3. _____
4. _____
5. _____
6. _____
7. _____
8. _____
9. _____
10. _____
11. _____
12. _____

13. _____
14. _____
15. _____
16. _____
17. _____
18. _____
19. _____
20. _____
21. _____
22. _____
23. _____
24. _____

Flushing Man: Lewis Latimer also made a great contribution near and dear to me (and the Four P's). In 1874, he and another inventor patented an improvement for toilets on railroad cars.

And, get this, he lived the last 25 years of his life in Flushing, NY. Flushing! Hee-hee. :-)

Year: 1894
Page: 84
Go Return

Jump to this page **or** follow the pipes.

1908 B-r-r-r, I've made my way to the cold forests of **Tunguska** in **Siberia, Russia**. A gigantic **explosion** has just taken place, creating one of the loudest noises in history. It was heard 1,000 miles away—that's like being in **New York** and hearing something that happened in **Florida**!

The Tunguska Event

Let's start with how to pronounce that name. It's Toon-goo-ska.

I've made a drawing to show what it looks like around here. Those lines in the circle are **trees** without branches, like a forest of **telephone poles**. The explosion happened right above them, tearing their branches off.

And all those little lines pointing away from the telephone-pole forest? Those are **tens of millions** of other trees that were knocked down from the blast—for 20 miles in all directions! The blast was so strong it sent **shock waves** around the world.

The **flames** in the drawing show the fire that resulted. It was so bright, the nighttime sky in **England**, thousands of miles away, glowed pink.

What caused the Tunguska Event? Some wild explanations were suggested. A crashing **alien spaceship**. **Ogdy**, a storm god to the local people, was angry. A "death ray" experiment by **Nikola Tesla** (read more about him on page 12).

But I like to be a little more scientific, and the explanation most experts agree on is that an **asteroid** or **comet** (a chunk of space rock or ice) came flying toward Earth and exploded about three miles (5 km) above the ground. That would explain why there's no big **crater** here.

But bits of the object should have been shot into the ground. Over the years, scientists have explored the area a number of times, but found no clear answers. It's still something of a mystery.

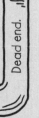
Dead end.

An explosion like the Tunguska Event is powerful enough to destroy a city such as Los Angeles or New York.

iPuzzle
Asteroids

The words below are spelled using the letters in ASTEROIDS.
There's only one way to fit all of them into each puzzle.
Counting the number of letters will help you.

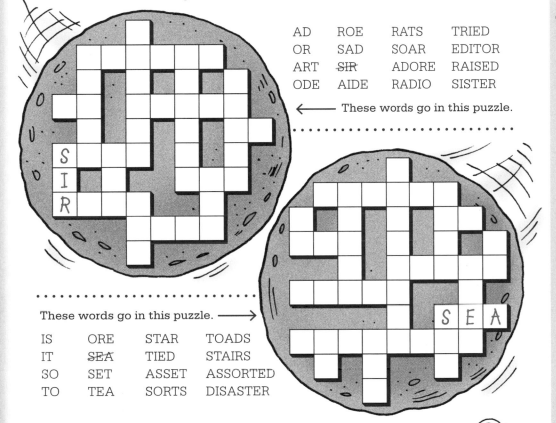

AD	ROE	RATS	TRIED
OR	SAD	SOAR	EDITOR
ART	~~SIR~~	ADORE	RAISED
ODE	AIDE	RADIO	SISTER

← These words go in this puzzle.

These words go in this puzzle. →

IS	ORE	STAR	TOADS
IT	~~SEA~~	TIED	STAIRS
SO	SET	ASSET	ASSORTED
TO	TEA	SORTS	DISASTER

Hard to Get to: It took 19 years before an expedition made it to Tunguska to look at the damage. That's because it's in the middle of nowhere. No highways, no towns, no stores. Just reindeer, bears, forests, swamps, and a few native people. In the winter, it gets really, really cold. In the short, hot summers, the air swarms with mosquitoes and biting flies.

Jump to this page **or** follow the pipes.

The Tunguska explosion was a million times louder than a clap of thunder.

1816

It's taken seven years, but the **French Academy of Sciences** finally has a winner for their **math contest**. It's...

Sophie Germain

Sophie Germain was a shy girl who fell in love with math at the age of 13. The **French Revolution** had just started, and the streets of **Paris** outside her home were a dangerous place. So Sophie began exploring her father's library.

A chapter in one book, *History of Mathematics*, really caught her attention. It told of the Greek mathematician **Archimedes** when his town was being attacked by the **Romans**. He was so involved with a math problem that he ignored a soldier's questions, who then killed him. That could have described Sophie's newfound love of math. Soon, she was reading everything in sight, often late into the night. Her parents tried to discourage her at first. They didn't think a girl should be spending all her time reading. But there was no stopping Sophie, so they finally gave in.

Five years later, a math and science **university** opened nearby. Sophie got some of the **lecture notes** from a male friend who was a student there. When he left for the war, she used his name to submit a paper for one course. It was so good, the teacher, **Joseph-Louis Lagrange**, wanted to meet the author. He was amazed to discover it was a teenage girl.

Germain continued working with Lagrange, and she communicated with other top mathematicians as well. **Carl Gauss**, one of the world's great math minds, praised her "extraordinary talents and superior genius."

In 1809, **Napoleon**, the emperor of France, suggested a prize be awarded to the person who could mathematically explain **Ernst Chladni's** vibrating plate demonstrations (see next page). It was a really difficult problem, one that would require new ideas and a ton of work—the perfect challenge for Sophie Germain.

Two years later, she sent in the contest's only entry. But she'd made some errors. So the contest was extended. Two years later, her 100-page entry was again the only one. It still wasn't quite right, but she received an **honorable mention** for her novel approach. Finally, on her third attempt, the contest committee awarded her the *prix extraordinaire* (grand prize)!

iPuzzle
Chladni Plates

In 1808, Ernst Chladni performed an amazing demonstration in Paris. He sprinkled sand on a glass plate and then "played" the edge of the glass with a violin bow. The grains of sand danced on the vibrating plate and lined up in complicated patterns. The patterns would change depending on where he held the plate and how he positioned the bow.

For this puzzle, find the two Chladni Plates that are exactly the same.

Most Difficult Ever: There was a math problem that was first suggested in 1637 and wasn't solved until 1995. That's 358 years of trying! Pierre de Fermat, a French lawyer, came up with the problem, which was named for him: Fermat's Last Theorem. Sophie Germain couldn't solve the problem, but she contributed a big breakthrough. Her new approach helped move things forward for future solvers.

Jump to this page **or** follow the pipes.

Germain taught herself Latin so she could read books written in that language by some of the great minds of the day.

Sophie was born on April Fools' Day in 1776, the year the U.S. Declaration of Independence was signed.

1973 Welcome to Tennessee's **Oak Ridge National Laboratory**. The scientists here have been trying to make a safer, cleaner type of **nuclear power** for about 20 years. But their project is being shut down.

Nuclear: Unclear

Let's make this simple because my eyes glaze over when someone tries to explain how nuclear power works. Here goes—a nuclear power plant splits **uranium atoms**, which produces **energy**, which boils **water**, which turns giant **turbines** (engines), which creates **electricity**.

The really great thing about nuclear power is it's clean. No **smoke** or **gases** belching into the sky. The really bad thing is that uranium is dangerous stuff. If there's an accident or you get too close to the **nuclear waste**, it'll fry you like a piece of bacon. Ouch! :-(

But the brainiacs here at Oak Ridge think they've found a better way. They're using **thorium** instead of uranium. It's not as dangerous to handle, it doesn't create as much waste, and there's lots of it.

So why not use thorium? There are a few reasons. First, uranium plants have been up and running for many years. Switching to something new takes a lot of time and money. Second, there's still some work to be done to perfect a thorium design. Third, uranium creates **plutonium**, which can be used to make powerful **bombs**. The **military** likes that. During the '50s and '60s, the U.S. and the U.S.S.R. were in a nuclear bomb-making race.

On the other hand, some people think any kind of nuclear power is a bad idea. They'd rather see more **green energy** being used, such as sun and wind power. In the 21st century (when you're reading this), there will be some big projects built: a **wind farm** in India, **solar towers** in Spain, and **geyser-powered plants** near San Francisco.

What do I think? Hey, remember, I'm a rat who gets flushed through sewer pipes! The important question is: What do *you* think?

Thorium is almost as common as lead and three to four times as common as uranium.

iPuzzle
Energy Anagrams

UNCLEAR is an anagram of NUCLEAR. It uses the same letters, but in a different order. Can you match up each phrase in the left column with a goofy anagram of it in the right column? Write the letters in the blanks.

1. ____ WIND FARM
2. ____ THORIUM
3. ____ SOLAR ENERGY
4. ____ PETROLEUM
5. ____ GEOTHERMAL
6. ____ NUCLEAR POWER
7. ____ ETHANOL
8. ____ NATURAL GAS
9. ____ BOILING WATER
10. ____ COAL MINE
11. ____ HYDROELECTRIC
12. ____ BIOMASS

A. GREASY LONER
B. LEMUR POET
C. LASAGNA RUT
D. FIRM WAND
E. GOBLIN WAITER
F. EMAIL CON
G. HUMOR IT
H. WEAPON CURLER
I. MISS BOA
J. CORRECTLY HIDE
K. GAMER HOTEL
L. HOT LANE

I'm no cat, and that's that.

Energy Dictionary: Terms from the puzzle above.

Petroleum: stuff pumped out of the earth and turned into heating oil and gasoline • **Geothermal energy:** power using heat from the earth (hot springs, geysers, etc.) • **Ethanol:** fuel made from corn to power cars • **Hydroelectric:** type of energy from a dam • **Biomass:** crops used for energy (by burning or rotting)

Year: 1973 Page: 26

Jump to this page **or** follow the pipes.

Heat from the earth accounts for 87% of Iceland's total heating needs.

Nuclear power plants provided about 12 percent of the world's electricity in 2011.

1992 I've come aboard the *Ever Laurel*, a ship heading from **Hong Kong** to the **U.S.** A huge storm is pounding it with wind and waves, and a big **container** has just fallen overboard. It's filled with 28,800…

Friendly Floatees

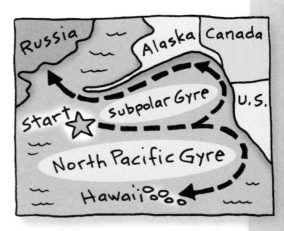

Friendly Floatees are plastic **bathtub toys**. They come in four types: yellow **ducks**, green **frogs**, blue **turtles**, and red **beavers**. The container broke open when it hit the water, and the Floatees were free!

A year later, some of the escaped toys began washing up on the shores of **Alaska**, 2,000 miles (3,200 km) from where they went overboard. That excited ocean experts, local newspapers, and driftologists (people who collect things washed up on beaches). A scientist at **NOAA**, the National Oceanic and Atmospheric Administration, used a **computer** to plot routes the Floatees might take. Articles and ads appeared about the toys. People started searching beaches. Over the next few years, more Floatees were sighted on **Alaskan shores**. They were also found in **Russia, Washington State**, and **Hawaii**.

Helping the Floatees on their journey were two large areas in the ocean called **gyres**. A gyre is a huge rotating patch of water. It's kind of like a flushing toilet bowl, except gentler, and the water doesn't go down.

The **Subpolar Gyre** sent some Floatees up the Alaska coast and around toward Russia. The **North Pacific Gyre** sent others down the American coast and then over for a vacation in beautiful Hawaii.

About 10 years later, there were **reports** that two Floatee ducks had made their

way across the **Arctic Ocean** into the **Atlantic**. Two people in **Maine** claimed they found one, but they hadn't kept the duck, so there was no proof. The second duck landed on an English beach, but it turned out to be made by a different company.

iPuzzle
Splash Match

Can you find the two water splashes that are identical in size and shape?

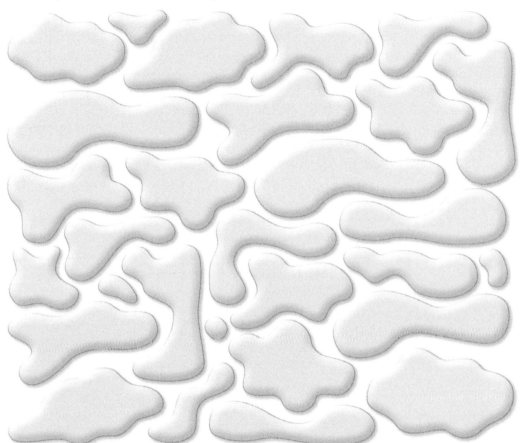

Great Pacific Garbage Patch: That's the name given to an area of the Pacific Ocean where floating garbage collects in large amounts. Friendly Floatees aren't alone — there are tons of other garbage in the ocean. Most of it is plastic, such as bottles and jars. But there are also fishing floats, ropes, nets, cans, crates, paper, shoes, and flip-flops.

Jump to this page **or** follow the pipes.

1914 I've flushed myself to the fourth floor of a **beauty salon** in **New York City**. You might think **chemistry** and **makeup** don't have much in common. They do when the makeup is made by **Elizabeth Arden**.

The Beauty Biz

Elizabeth Arden first got the idea of making beauty products when she was a nursing student in **Canada**. She saw a **chemist** working on a **skin salve** and thought something like that could be used as a **face cream** for women. That was kind of a new idea. In 1900, the only people who wore makeup were actors.

Arden dropped out of school and turned her family's kitchen into a beauty potion lab. Unfortunately, the only thing she succeeded at making were awful odors that stunk up the **neighborhood**. The **melted fats** she used smelled like rotten eggs! (Hee-hee.) Her father shut things down and told her to get a job. She did.

A few years later, Arden moved to **New York City**. At a medical drug company where she worked, she met some more chemists. She grilled them for information and started experimenting with skin products again. It went much better this time. People didn't have to hold their noses! :-) She used her new creations in a **beauty salon** she opened in 1910.

But Arden wanted even better products. So she took a trip to **Paris** and visited every beauty salon she could find. A month later, she returned home with a suitcase stuffed full of the creams and lotions she'd collected.

She then hired a chemist, **A. Fabian Swanson**, to find out what was in the products. After he'd done that, she gave him the job of creating a "face cream that was light and fluffy, almost like whipped cream." It took him several months, but the cream, which Arden named **Venetian Cream Amoretta**, was a big hit.

More successes followed, and Arden soon became one of the richest women in the world. All it took was a dream, a ton of hard work, and a bit of chemistry.

Face Goop Industrial strength

Ardena

Elizabeth Arden was born Florence Nightingale Graham, but she changed her name to match the name of her beauty salon.

iPuzzle
Lipstick on the Loose

Traveling on the lipstick lines, find a route from START to END.

start

End

Delivery Problems: A. Fabian Swanson's lab was downtown, far from Arden's salon. At first, he delivered gallon jugs of the products himself using city trains. But as business grew, the vats became bigger and bigger. He was getting worn out! So Arden got a truck, and Swanson's lugging days were over.

Year: 1931
Page: 80

Jump to this page **or** follow the pipes.

1801

We're in **London, England**, at the lock store of **Joseph Bramah**. He's just posted a sign in the window offering a reward to anyone who can open his ...

Unpickable Lock

Here's what the sign says:

The Artist who can make an Instrument that will pick or Open this Lock shall Receive 200 Guineas The Moment it is produced.

← 4 inches →

That's actually a lot of money. If you won it in 2012, that would be over $15,000.

Locks have been used for thousands of years. Early ones used **rope** tied in knots. The ancient **Egyptians** made wooden locks and keys 4,000 years ago. The **Romans** later used metal. Locks are even mentioned in the Bible.

For 50 years, Bramah's lock remained unopened. There were 18 **sliders** (flat iron pieces) inside the lock, each with a series of notches. To open the lock, the notches had to line up just right. But there were at least a trillion different ways they could be positioned. That meant you could try a million different ways every day for a million days (2,700 years) before finding the solution!

However, that didn't stop an American lock salesman named **Alfred C. Hobbs** from opening it in 1851. He'd come to London to show off his company's new lock. Having discovered that picking the competition's locks helped sales, Hobbs took up the Bramah challenge. No, he didn't try a trillion different ways. Using his **locksmith tools**, he felt around inside and made measurements. It took him 44 hours spread out over 10 days, but he finally succeeded.

And, boy, did that cause a ruckus. Banks that were using the lock panicked. The **Bramah lock company** claimed he'd cheated. Instead of using a single instrument (as stated in their original window sign), he'd used two **needles**, one curved at the end, and a small **steel rod** held by a **clamp**. London newspapers followed every detail, calling it the **Great Lock Controversy**. Finally, a **jury** ruled in Hobbs' favor, and the 200-guinea prize was his.

Dead end.

In the 1770s, Bramah had a job installing toilets in London homes.

iPuzzle
Pick a Lock

These ropes have been locked together. But they can all be separated by unlocking just one lock. Which one is it?

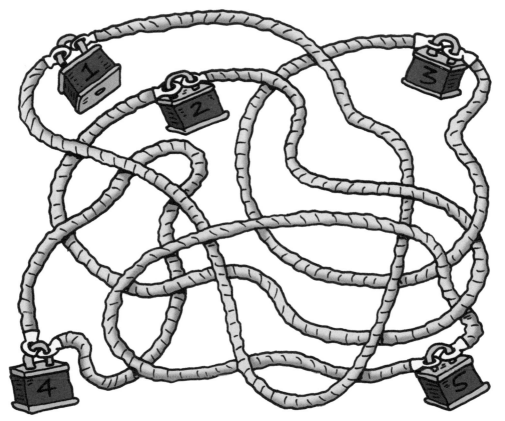

Dart Lock: Made in 1840, the Peirce Identifying Detector Lock used an unusual idea. If anything other than the correct key was used to try to open the lock, a dart would shoot out from below the keyhole. It not only hurt, but it also left a identifying stamp on the thief's wrist for weeks. No more guessing who the crook was. He'd be caught red-handed…er, red-wristed.

Jump to this page **or** follow the pipes.

An English locksmith tried to pick a lock that Hobbs designed, but failed.

2007 I've iSwirled myself to a large open-pit **coal mine** in **Colombia**, **South America**. Scientists have just dug up some fossilized **Titanoboa** bones, a 58-million-year-old...

Sssuper Sssnake!

Let's start with the size of this snake, because I can hardly believe it. Titanoboa weighed 2,500 pounds and measured 48 feet long (1,135 kg and 15 m). That's the weight of a small **car** and the length of a large **bus**!

Let me explain it another way, because I want to make sure you have a good picture of just how huge this slithering monster was. Go to a doorway in your home or school. Imagine a snake so wide it has to squeeze through the opening! Now, go round up eight adults and have them lie down, head to toe one after the other. That's how long Titanoboa was! Add another five adults, and that's how much Titanoboa weighed!

Okay, I'm done. Pretty amazing, huh?

Titanoboa lived in a **tropical rainforest,** spending most of its time in the water. Other **reptile** neighbors included **half-ton crocodiles**, which Titanoboa could swallow whole, and giant **turtles** the size of cafeteria tables.

Why was Titanoboa so big? Snakes are **coldblooded**, which means they need heat from the air to keep their bodies warm. And the larger they are, the more heat it takes (just like it takes more heat to warm up a big **sausage**, compared to a little one). Some scientists estimate the tropical rainforests were as much as 10° F (5.5° C) warmer then than they are today. So the warmer air made it possible for **Titanoboa** to grow larger.

Snake Reward

In 1912, President Teddy Roosevelt and the Bronx Zoo offered a $1,000 reward to anyone who captured a snake longer than 30 feet. The amount has since been upped to $50,000, but no one has claimed the prize. The longest known snake in modern times was a 28-foot python.

iPuzzle
Sssnake Sssearch

Look for each snake either forward, backward, up, down, or diagonally.

ADDER
ANACONDA
BOA
COBRA
COPPERHEAD
COTTONMOUTH
DIAMONDHEAD
GARTER
HOGNOSE
KEELBACK
KRAIT
MAMBA
PYTHON
RATTLER
SERPENT
SIDEWINDER
VIPER

```
D T N E P R E S Q V W Z
I D U O K C A B L E E K
A A E Z H O G N O S E F
M E R A T T L E R R R P
O H E A C T Y D V E E P
N R T Z D O D P F D P L
D E R E D N I W E D I S
H P A B H M O V N A V T
E P G N A O L C O B R A
A O J M Y U K R A I T X
D C B O A T D B H N M Y
D A Z X X H D U M N A O
```

The Cerrejón open-pit coal mine, where Titanoboa was found, is the size of Chicago.

Titanoboa females were much larger than the males. The same is true of many snakes today.

What do snakes study in school?

Why couldn't the snake talk?

How would you describe Titanoboa?

Hiss-tory.

It had a frog in its throat.

Unarmed but dangerous.

Jump to this page **or** follow the pipes.

Modern-day relatives of Titanoboa are the boa constrictor and the anaconda.

1631 We're in **Lima, Peru**, where a **Jesuit priest** is packing for a trip to **Rome**. One of his bags contains a small supply of something that will change medicine—**cinchona tree bark**.

The Fever Tree

A cinchona tree on a Peruvian coin

In the 1600s, Rome had a terrible problem with a disease called **malaria**. Many people died from it. Tons more suffered terribly from the fever, aches, and stomach problems that came with it.

Doctors thought malaria was caused by bad fluids in the body. To get rid of the fluids, they'd **bleed** their patients (cut them), give them **sneezing powder**, and use medicines that made them…well, have to run to the bathroom.

People who couldn't afford doctors tried other methods. One way was hanging an orange with a **peach pit** inside it around the neck. Another was bringing a **sheep** into the sick person's bedroom, hoping the fever would be transferred to the animal. Sounds like a baaad idea. :-)

But the cure for malaria turned out to be in the red bark of a tree found clear across the **Atlantic Ocean** in the **Andean Mountains**. The **Quechua people** there had been using it for hundreds of years as a cure for shivering.

In 1605, a Jesuit monk named **Agustino Salumbrino** sailed from Italy to Peru. When he learned about the cinchona tree bark, he wondered if it might work on malaria. He sent a supply of it back to Rome, and it did!

More tree bark shipments followed, and the use of **quinine** (powder made from the bark) slowly spread across **Europe**. It also played a part in changing the way doctors looked at disease. The idea of draining the body of bad fluids—a practice that had been followed for 2,000 years—soon faded away.

Happy Mosquito Day!

In 1897, Sir Ronald Ross, a British army doctor, proved that malaria was spread by mosquitoes. In honor of his discovery, World Mosquito Day is celebrated every year on August 20.

Jesuits are members of a religious order of the Roman Catholic Church.

The word "quinine" comes from "kina," the Quechuan word for bark.

iPuzzle
Quinine Nine

Look for nine differences between these two cinchona drawings.

This illustration is from *Köhler's Medicinal Plants,* published in 1887.

It was drawn by Walther Müller.

Fever War: In 1809, the British were worried about a fleet of ships Napoleon had in Holland. That summer, they sent 40,000 troops to the island of Walcheren to deal with it. After they set up camp, Napoleon ordered a dyke broken, flooding the area. A month later, 8,200 British soldiers were feverish with malaria, and 250 were dying every week. In December, the British pulled out, defeated not by bullets, but by mosquitoes and malaria.

Jump to this page **or** follow the pipes.

Bathroom Break

Listen, I know you're still in the middle of your **Interpipe** adventure. But I could use a break. I'm starting to get a little soggy.

Tell the truth.

You didn't think I was gonna be as smart as I am, did you? I mean, who ever heard of a rat who could learn about **200-year-old locks**. Or an **Assyrian palace** from 3,000 years ago. Or how **English shepherds** decorated their sheep.

Impressive, huh? Well, I'm impressed.

How'd a lab rat get so brainy?

I don't spend all my time getting flushed down toilets. I've got a lot of spare time, and the Four P's have put together a pretty cool **library** next to the **lab**. I like to spend hours in there turning myself into a more educated rodent.

It's amazing the things that **humans** have done over the years. Reading never fails to get me thinking and dreaming and coming up with ideas. It's like traveling to different places and different times—but without the smelly **sewer pipes**!

The Four P's.

You're probably wondering about the **Four P's**. They're a pretty secretive group, but here are a few things I can tell you.

Plumb Bob: He graduated from college with a master's degree in **sewerology**, which is as high as it gets in the plumbing world. He likes **cats** and hates **asparagus**. That's why there's no mention of asparagus in this book. Oh! Oops. :-(

Phyllis Tanks: With a name like Tanks, she decided to make toilet tanks her life. Her favorite color is yellow, which kinda makes sense in her line of work. When she's not around, we all say, "No Tanks!"

P. Liddy: He was born into a family of **plumbers** and raised in the town of **Sooher, Maine**. He's a wizard with an adjustable **pipe wrench**, which he carries on his belt at all times. Nobody knows what the "P" stands for. Mysterious, huh?

Portia Potty: Potty grew up in **France** but came to **America** where the real toilet opportunities were. She soon learned not to say "oui, oui," which means "yes, yes" in French, because it sounds like "wee wee" in English.

Okay, back to work.

I've taken a deep breath, so turn the page whenever you're ready!

Jump to this page **or** follow the pipes.

1865

The Four P's have insisted I visit **Gregor Mendel** in **Moravia** (now the **Czech Republic**). This is where Mendel spent years growing **peas**. That's right, peas! Do you see now why the Four P's like him?

Give Peas a Chance

Science isn't always about finding dinosaur bones or watching meteors streak across the sky. Sometimes it's really **dull work**. Like spending a day counting 7,324 peas!

Gregor Mendel, a monk at the **Abbey of St. Thomas**, actually did that. And not just for one day. Over a **seven-year period**, he grew tens of thousands of **pea plants**, counted hundreds of thousands of peas, and filled up page after page in his **notebooks** keeping track of all those peas. A pea nut, you could say. :-)

Why? Mendel wondered what would happen if he crossed two different pea plants. He figured he'd get an in-between kind of plant. But that's not what happened. When he crossed plants that had **yellow pods** with plants that had **green pods**, he got only plants with **green pods**. No yellow pods and no yellowish green pods. Just green, green, green!

He did more **experiments**, using plants of different heights, with different seeds, and different flowers. But he always got plants of one height, with one kind of seed, and one kind of flower. These pea plants were stubborn!

Mendel finally figured out why this was happening and gave a lecture to a group of scientists and professors. He explained that peas have permanent **traits**, some of which are stronger than others. For example, the green-pod trait was stronger than the yellow-pod trait, which is why he got only plants with green pods.

That was an amazing discovery. It's one of the basic ideas behind the branch of biology known as **genetics**. But do you know what kind of response Mendel got? Zip! Some polite applause, then the audience ran for the exits. The only exception was one scientist who wrote Mendel later to tell him he was wrong. :-(

Luckily, 35 years later, several scientists found printed copies of Mendel's lecture and realized what he'd done. They let the world know about his work, and the field of genetics was off and running.

Mendel noted the weather in his notebook three times a day, every day, for the last 27 years of his life!

Although his work was totally ignored during his lifetime, Mendel once said, "My time will come."

iPuzzle
The Four Peas

Look for four peas in a row that are the same color. There are
four such groups, each group being either all light or all dark peas.
Each group runs in a straight line either across, down, or diagonally.

To make sure bees wouldn't ruin his experiments, Mendel put little covers over the flowers on his pea plants.

Wake Up! What did Mendel do with all those peas after
he'd grown and counted them? He wasn't just a gardener. He
also taught science at a high school, and the story goes that
he used to fill his pockets with peas before class.
Then, if he caught any students sleeping, he'd
throw peas at their heads to wake them up!

bonk

Year: 1876
Page: 76
Go Darwin

Jump to this
page **or** follow
the pipes.

250 We're in **Mesopotamia** (now Iraq), where I've tracked down an unusual **clay jar** known as ...

The Baghdad Battery

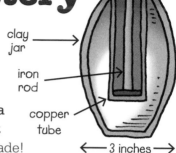

stopper

clay jar

iron rod

copper tube

←— 3 inches —→

In the 1930s, when this jar was dug up, people wondered what it was. An **archaeologist** (an expert on old objects) named **William König** had an idea. He thought it was a **battery**. If true, that would be an incredible discovery. **Alessandro Volta** had been credited with inventing the battery—but that happened over 1,500 years after this jar was made!

Other archaeologists doubted König's claim. They said the **Parthians**, the people who lived here when the jar was made, had no knowledge of electricity. They felt the jar was more likely used for storing **sacred scrolls**.

Leyden jar

When you look at the design of this curious object, you can see why König thought what he did. Inside the jar is a **copper tube** with an **iron rod** in it. A plug at the top of the jar holds everything in place. It looks sort of like a **Leyden jar**, invented in 1745, but that device only collects electricity. König thought the Baghdad battery could produce electricity if it were filled with a **mild acid** such as grape juice or vinegar.

An **experiment** was done in 1940, filling a similar jar with acid, and it produced electricity! It wasn't very powerful—it would take six Baghdad batteries to power one **TV remote control**—but it worked.

So we're left with a couple of questions. Is it really a battery? Or is it something that just happens to be usable as a battery, knowing what we know now?

Truth Hurts

In 2005, the Discovery Channel's show *Mythbusters* made their own Baghdad batteries. Connecting ten jars together allowed them to coat a piece of copper with zinc, and also to create some painful little jolts.

Dead end.

Volta's battery stacked up alternating layers of zinc, brine-soaked cardboard, and copper.

LED light bulb

alligator clip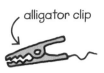

iPuzzle
Lemon "Juice"

We've made batteries using lemons (instructions below).
Follow the wires from lemon to lemon to get from START to END.

Parthian soldiers were known as great horsemen and archers.

Lemon Battery: Roll a lemon until it's squishy inside. Push a copper penny (it has to be a shiny one) and a zinc-coated screw (the shiny silvery kind) halfway in. You now have a battery! Increase the power by attaching several lemon batteries together using wires and alligator clips (found in hardware stores). Attach a screw in one lemon to a penny in another, as shown. Touch the end wires to an LED (low voltage light bulb), and it'll glow.

Jump to this page **or** follow the pipes.

1949

N. Joseph Woodland and his friend Bernard Silver have just filed a patent for the Classifying Apparatus and Method. You might know it better as a…

Bar Code

Those rectangles of thick and thin black lines on just about every product you buy are **bar codes**. When a cashier scans one, it tells the **cash register** what the item is and how much it costs. That scanned information is then sent to the store's main computer to track what's been sold.

In 1948, Silver overheard a **supermarket executive** talking about the need for a **product coding system**. He set to work with his pal Woodland, and they came up with an idea using **ink patterns** that glowed under a special light. But the ink faded quickly, and the lights were expensive.

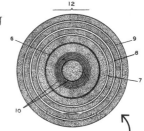

The drawing from their patent

Woodland was convinced they were on the right track. He moved into his grandfather's home in **Miami Beach** and spent the winter working on a different approach. The result was a **circular bar code** that would read the same from any direction. The printed code worked well, but the device for reading the code was the size of a desk! It also used a 500-watt light bulb that could catch paper on fire.

It was 20 years before two inventions came along that made Woodland's bar code usable — the **laser scanner** and small cheap **computers**. After grocery-store testing in 1972, the bar code was changed to the rectangular shape we now know. That design is called a **UPC** (Universal Product Code).

Woodland's original circular design is known as a bull's-eye bar code.

• The black lines and white spaces represent numbers (the 12 numbers at the bottom).

• Every UPC starts and ends with two skinny black lines separated by a skinny white space.

• The lines are for scanners, the numbers for humans.

WHAT'S IN A UPC?

0 54000 20042 7

• What the numbers mean:

0 = general category

54000 = the company that made the product

20042 = the exact product

7 = what the computer uses to double-check its scan (Don't ask, it's complicated!)

The UPC above is from a roll of Scott toilet paper.

iPuzzle
Bar Code Jokes

We've written the answers to these jokes using a special iFlush Labs bar code. Figure out how the code works. Then write the correct letter in each blank.

1. ___ Where do hamburgers go to dance?

2. ___ What do you call a cow that tilts?

3. ___ What has two eyes, a big bottom, and waves all the time?

4. ___ What room can't zombies enter?

5. ___ What did zero say to eight?

6. ___ How do you get straight A's?

A.

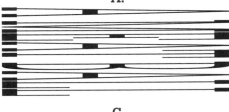

B.

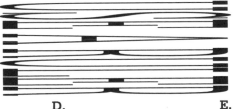

C.

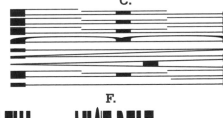

D.

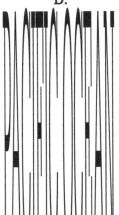

E.

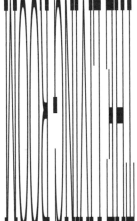

F.

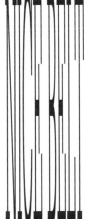

Jump to this page **or** follow the pipes.

1854

Florence Nightingale has just arrived in a **British army hospital** in **Turkey**. It's a mess, but Flo is on the job!

A Rare Bird

England was at war with **Russia** on the **Crimean peninsula**. That's on the **Black Sea** in southern Russia. A British **military hospital** was set up across the sea in Turkey, but it was filthy, overcrowded, and lacking in supplies. Many more soldiers were dying from **disease** than from **battle wounds**!

Something had to be done, and the Secretary of War had an idea. He asked **Florence Nightingale**, a woman he'd known for years, if she'd lead a team of nurses into the war zone. Nightingale had devoted her life to caring for the sick and suffering, a calling she said she'd received from God as a teenager. She immediately agreed.

1855 drawing of Nightingale from *Punch* magazine

Nightingale threw herself into the task. She cleaned up the **hospital** and **patients**, attended **surgeries**, and arranged for better food. (Go, Flo!) If a soldier was in worse shape than an officer, he'd be taken care of first. (Move aside, General! Hee-hee.) Late into the night, using a lamp to light her way, Nightingale went from bed to bed doing whatever she could. (Her nickname was "The Lady with the Lamp.") The soldiers loved her, and newspapers soon made her the most famous woman in **Europe**.

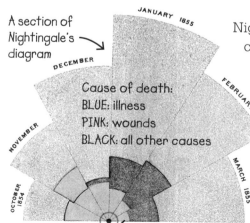

A section of Nightingale's diagram

JANUARY 1855
DECEMBER
FEBRUARY
NOVEMBER
OCTOBER 1854
MARCH 1855

Cause of death:
BLUE: illness
PINK: wounds
BLACK: all other causes

Nightingale's most lasting contributions came after the war. Her ideas, detailed reports, and **diagrams** (see drawing) fueled changes made within the army's **medical department**. She also created the model for the **modern nurse** and was the inspiration for the **Red Cross**, formed in 1863.

← Each colored wedge starts at the center point.

iPuzzle
Flo's Challenge

At age 8, Florence Nightingale (nicknamed Flo) wrote her sister: "Here is a game for you. Take any word and see how many words you can make out of the letters. I took BREATH and made 40 words." Can you match Florence? Words can be of any length. Getting even 20 words is cracking (that's good).

BREATH

1. _____	11. _____	21. _____	31. _____
2. _____	12. _____	22. _____	32. _____
3. _____	13. _____	23. _____	33. _____
4. _____	14. _____	24. _____	34. _____
5. _____	15. _____	25. _____	35. _____
6. _____	16. _____	26. _____	36. _____
7. _____	17. _____	27. _____	37. _____
8. _____	18. _____	28. _____	38. _____
9. _____	19. _____	29. _____	39. _____
10. _____	20. _____	30. _____	40. _____

EXTRA CREDIT: Here's another word game from Flo's letter. Take the phrase GREAT HELP and rearrange the letters into one word. Warning: It's a means of communication that was used in Flo's time, but isn't used much today.

Flo's Day: Every day as a young child, Flo would draw an object, practice the piano, do needlework, walk, and exercise several times. She memorized poems, read the Bible, studied French, and kept track of her money. On Sundays, she'd often write a summary of the church sermon.

Jump to this page **or** follow the pipes.

A charged atom is an *ion*. The negative end of a battery is an *anode*.

1834

You might think the word **scientist** has been around for as long as there have been science-type people. Not so! **William Whewell** came up with the term less than 200 years ago.

Scientist

Science originally meant knowledge. It later came to mean knowledge that could be seen and demonstrated. People who dabbled in science in the early days, people like **Sir Isaac Newton** and **Archimedes**, were called **natural philosophers**.

William Whewell was a natural philosopher himself. He was also a writer with a knack for creating new scientific words. He invented the terms **ion** and **anode** for his friend, the electromagnetic whiz **Michael Faraday**. He also dreamed up the words **Eocene** and **Miocene** for two long-ago time periods.

By the 1800s, science had branched off in many directions, and Whewell thought there should be one **word** to cover everyone who was involved in it. *Savans*, a French word meaning "wise one," was his first thought. But that seemed a bit too lofty. *Naturforscher*, a German word meaning "nature investigator," was another possibility. But he worried people might translate it as "nature peeper." He finally settled on **scientist**.

Whewell's first use of the word scientist appeared in an 1834 issue of the British publication *Quarterly Review*, but there was little reaction. In 1840, he wrote a book and brought it up again. "We need very much a name to describe a cultivator of science in general. I should incline to call him a *Scientist*. Thus we might say, that as an Artist is a Musician, Painter, or Poet, a Scientist is a Mathematician, Physicist, or Naturalist," he wrote.

Faraday thought that seemed fine but griped about another new word Whewell had thrown in—**physicist**. That was the kind of scientist Faraday was. He thought the three "i" sounds made the word "so awkward that I think I shall never be able to use it." He didn't, and he never used the term **scientist** either! Faraday and others continued to call themselves **natural philosophers**. But as these holdouts died out, so too did objections to the word scientist.

Whewell was an expert on astronomy, physics, geology, architecture, math, religion, economics, and many other subjects.

iPuzzle
What's That Mean?

Each word in the left column has an anagram in the right column (all the same letters in a different order). Next to the correct anagram is a definition of the left-column word.

1. ___ ZODIOGRAPHER

2. ___ PHOSPHENE

3. ___ AEROLITH

4. ___ THAGOMIZER

5. ___ PETRICHOR

6. ___ ERUCTATION

7. ___ MICTURATION

8. ___ STERNUTATION

9. ___ JUMENTOUS

10. ___ KONISCOPE

11. ___ PERISTEROPHILE

12. ___ BORBORYGMUS

13. ___ MYTACISM

14. ___ BROMHIDROSIS

15. ___ FORMICATION

16. ___ MASTICATION

17. ___ SOMNAMBULIST

18. ___ PHALANGES

19. ___ PEDUNCLE

20. ___ ANTITRAGUS

A. EARTH GIZMO - stegosaurus tail spikes

B. JOUST MENU - smelling like horse pee

C. OH, RIPE REPTILES - pigeon collector

D. GRUBBY ROOMS - stomach growling

E. ANT GUITARS - the little lump on a human ear just above the ear lobe

F. CAT ROUTINE - burping

G. CLUED PEN - flower stalk

H. SICKO PEON - instrument for measuring dust in the air

I. ROAM FICTION - feeling of ants crawling on one's skin

J. MISTY MAC - Overuse of the letter "m"

K. RETRO CHIP - smell of rain on dry ground

L. HEP PHONES - light seen when the eyeball is gently pressed with the eyelid closed

M. AIR HOTEL - a stone that falls from the sky

N. PLANE HAGS - finger or toe bones

O. HIS BIRD ROOMS - body odor

P. SUMO LAB MINTS - sleepwalker

Q. INSTANT ROUTE - sneezing

R. HIP ZOO GRADER - one who writes about animals

S. ATOMIC STAIN - chewing

T. TRIM CAUTION - peeing

A newly coined word is called a NEOLOGISM. An anagram of that is GOON SMILE... or GNOME OILS.

Jump to this page **or** follow the pipes.

1776 I've come to **Connecticut** to check out a **submarine** designed by **David Bushnell** to sink **British ships** during the **American Revolution**.

The Turtle Sub

view of the sub from above

Bushnell's design was simple but clever. The submarine had two **propellers** and a **rudder** for steering. A **foot pedal** let water in to make the sub go down. The water could be pumped back out to **resurface**. Everything was operated by hand, so the pilot had to have strong arms!

The sub was made of two carved **tree trunk** pieces, held together by an **iron band**. Bushnell called it the *Turtle* because he thought it looked like two **tortoise shells** joined together.

brass tower with portholes all around and on top

drill for attaching bomb to enemy ship

air pipes

gunpowder keg

propeller to go up and down

depth gauge

propeller to go forward or backward

water inlet valve

water pump

rudder

water pump

lead weight

area fills with water for submerging

1875 drawings by Francis Barber

In September 1776, **General George Washington** authorized the *Turtle*'s first mission, an attempt to sink the British warship **HMS** *Eagle* in **New York City**'s harbor. **Sergeant Ezra Lee** volunteered to pilot the vessel. Once underwater, Lee couldn't see a thing, but he somehow managed to get beneath the *Eagle*. He started drilling into the ship's bottom to attach a keg of **gunpowder** to it. But the drill bit wouldn't go in. He must have hit an **iron plate**. Just then a **water current** caught the sub and sent it to the surface. Lee had to retreat, and the mission failed.

The *Turtle* was used for two other **missions**, but they failed, too. A month later, the sub was sunk in a battle on the **Hudson River** and never seen again.

Bushnell graduated from Yale in 1715, where he studied math and science.

When the *Turtle* went underwater, the air in it was good for only 30 minutes.

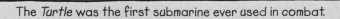

The *Turtle* was the first submarine ever used in combat.

iPuzzle
Turtle Doodles

Match the correct caption to each drawing.

When you're done, create your own turtle doodles.

1. ____

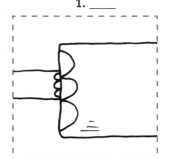

2. ____

3. ____

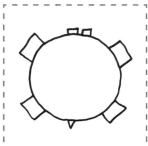

4. ____

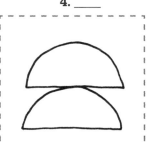

5. ____

6. ____

A. Shy turtle with buckteeth

B. A turtledove

C. Turtle asleep on a rock

D. Turtle wearing a turtleneck sweater

E. Turtle speedometer

F. Turtle and elephant shaking hands

Foxfire: There was no way of lighting the *Turtle* when it was used at night. The sub had a depth gauge and a compass, but how could the pilot see these instruments in the dark water? Bushnell came up with a clever solution—foxfire, a green-glowing fungus found in rotting wood. He put bits of foxfire on the depth gauge's floating cork. He also marked the compass points with it. Just one problem, foxfire only glowed in warm weather!

Jump to this page **or** follow the pipes.

George Washington, Thomas Jefferson, and Benjamin Franklin were consulted when Bushnell worked on his invention.

Dead end.

1811

I'm visiting a 12-year-old girl named **Mary Anning** who's just dug out the **skeleton** of an ancient *Ichthyosaurus*.

Fossil Hunter

Mary's love of hunting for **fossils** came from her father. The two would spend hours digging together in the seaside cliffs of **Lyme Regis** in southern **England**. When he died, Mary continued on her own, searching for ancient **rocks**, **bones**, and **shells** in the **limestone** and **shale**. She sold her finds to **tourists**. Her family was desperately poor, and Mary's fossil hunting was one of their few sources of money.

Ammonites (extinct spiral-shelled **mollusks)** were big sellers. But she'd never found anything like this skeleton. *Ichthyosaurus* had the mouth of a **crocodile**, the flippers of a **dolphin**, the backbone of a **fish**, and the chest of a **lizard**. The 17-foot-long **sea reptile** lived 175 million years in the past! Mary sold it to a **London museum** collector for 23 English **pounds**. That was enough money to feed her family for half a year.

Mary continued making daily visits to the cliffs, armed with a **hammer**, **chisel**, and the **pick** her father had made for her. Her knowledge of the creatures she found grew, as did her skill in removing them from the rock. **Scientists** would visit, not to share what they knew, but to learn from her.

Mary Anning made other astounding finds over the years, all firsts: ← *Plesiosaurus* (a huge sea reptile), *Dimorphodon* (a flying reptile), and *Squaloraja* (a sharklike fish). When Anning found dried ink sacs in **belemnites** (squidlike creatures), the local **artists** used the ink to create and sell **drawings** of the cliff's prehistoric creatures. She also discovered **coprolites** and figured out what they were—fossilized piles of **dung** (poop from ancient animals). That was important for knowing what they ate.

A Bright Child

At age one, Mary was in the arms of a woman when lightning hit a tree they were under. The woman and two others were killed, but Mary lived. Years later, neighbors claimed the incident had made her a much healthier, livelier child.

iPuzzle
Tongue Twisters

The tongue twister "She sells seashells on the seashore" was inspired by Mary Anning's life. Fill in the one word that best completes each of our tongue twisters below, then try saying the phrase three times fast. Each word will be used just once.

1. MULLING _____ OF MOLLUSKS

2. ANY ANNING _____ ANY AD

3. FEW _____ FRESH FISH FOSSILS

4. PICKS, SACKS, STICKS, _____ , ROCKS

5. DINOSAURS _____ ON SANDY SHORES

6. GUESTS _____ THE GEOLOGIST'S QUEST

7. REPTILES _____ WHILE LEOPARDS WEPT

8. LIMBER LIMBS _____ LYME CLIFFS

9. INSTINCTIVE SCIENTISTS _____

10. DOGS _____ DUNG DREGS

A. LEAPT

B. DIG

C. MILLIONS

D. INSIST

E. CLIMB

F. BLOCKS

G. FIND

H. GUESSED

I. SNORED

J. ANSWERED

She smells, she sells, she's sore.

Poo Table: An Oxford geology professor named William Buckland was a friend of Mary's. On one visit to Lyme Regis, Mary told him she thought some rocklike shapes she'd dug up were fossilized dung (coprolites). She was right, and Buckland was so excited with the discovery that he had a dining-room tabletop made using polished coprolites. Known as "Buckland's Dinosaur Poo Table," it's now on display at a museum in Lyme Regis.

Year: 1816
Page: 34
Go   Return

Jump to this page **or** follow the pipes.

The people of Lyme Regis would sometimes put bacon in their chimneys to keep witches away.

1911

The word **autism** was first used by the psychiatrist **Paul Bleuler** in 1911. But it was years before autism was better understood.

Different

the human brain →

Autistic people are born with **brains** that work differently than most people's. Understanding what others are feeling and, sometimes, what they mean can be a struggle. But some autistic people can perform incredible feats, such as quickly multiplying 37 x 37 x 37 x 37 x 37 in their heads. (It's 69,343,957.)

Temple Grandin is autistic. When she was young, other kids called her **Tape Recorder** because she kept saying the same things over and over. They teased her because she was different. But she went on to become a doctor of **animal science** and a professor at **Colorado State University**. In her book, *Animals in Translation*, Grandin wrote, "Autism made school and social life hard, but it made animals easy."

Daniel Tammet is an **autistic savant**, which means he has exceptional skills in certain areas. At age 13, after his father taught him the rules of **chess**, Daniel beat his dad in their very first game. Daniel also sees colors and images for every word he reads. That's helped him learn 10 **languages**—easily! Like Temple, Daniel didn't fit in at school. During recess he'd stand by himself in the trees next to the playground, unable to relate to the other kids. He was 11 before he made his first friend, a boy named **Babak**. This is what he said about Babak in his book, *Born on a Blue Day*: "He was the first person to make any real attempt to look past the things that made me different and instead focus on what we had in common: our love of words and numbers in particular."

Kim Peek (1951-2009) was a **mega-savant** who memorized huge amounts of information in more than a dozen subjects. He could read a book in an hour and then remember nearly everything in it, word for word. He was able to recall the contents of over 12,000 books. The movie *Rain Man* was inspired by Kim Peek. But Peek's one-of-a-kind brain had a flip side. He couldn't cook a meal or comb his own hair. Following directions or solving problems was very difficult. It was when reciting facts, which Peek usually did with a smile and a laugh, that he really shined.

iPuzzle
Prime Time

A prime number is any number greater than 1 that can be divided *only* by 1 and itself. Here's how to find the prime numbers below:

Start at the number 2 and cross off every second number (4, 6, 8, etc). Don't cross off 2. Next, start with 3 and cross off every third number (6, 9, 12, etc.). Skip 4 since it's already crossed off. Start at 5 and cross off every fifth number, then start at 7 and cross off every seventh number. The numbers that are left (not crossed off) are all the prime numbers.

To get things started, we've crossed out 1 and the first row of numbers for 2.

✖	2	3	✖	5	✖	7	✖	9	✖
11	12	13	14	15	16	17	18	19	20
21	22	23	24	25	26	27	28	29	30
31	32	33	34	35	36	37	38	39	40
41	42	43	44	45	46	47	48	49	50
51	52	53	54	55	56	57	58	59	60
61	62	63	64	65	66	67	68	69	70
71	72	73	74	75	76	77	78	79	80
81	82	83	84	85	86	87	88	89	90
91	92	93	94	95	96	97	98	99	100

Remember, don't cross off 2. Same thing for 3, 5, and 7.

A Piece of Pi: Pi is a math term for the distance around the outside of a circle (circumference) divided by the distance across the circle's middle (diameter). No matter what size circle, the answer is always the same, about 3.14. But pi's digits continue forever in a random order: 3.14159265359, and so on. In 2004, Daniel Tammet recited 22,514 digits of pi from memory without a mistake. It took him 5 hours and 9 minutes.

Year: 1914
Page: 40

Jump to this page **or** follow the pipes.

One of Daniel Tammet's interests is numbers, especially prime numbers. That's the inspiration for this puzzle.

This method for finding prime numbers (in the puzzle) is called the Sieve of Eratosthenes.

Two other scientists shared the Nobel Prize in chemistry with Molina — F. Sherwood Rowland and Paul Crutzen.

1995

We're in **Mexico City. Mario Molina** just got word he's won the **Nobel Prize** in **chemistry**, the highest honor in science.

MoLiNa ← chemical symbols for molybdenum, lithium, and sodium

It all started for **Mario** at age 10. He looked through a **toy microscope** and saw tiny **creatures** swimming around. He thought that was really cool. Encouraged by his **Aunt Esther**, who was a **chemist**, Mario got permission to turn an extra bathroom in his house into a **chemistry lab**. You heard me right—a lab in his bathroom! Our kinda guy. :-)

Mario tried to interest his friends in his **experiments**. But they preferred playing outside to hanging out in a bathroom. So he worked alone or, sometimes, with his aunt. She helped him set up experiments college students would do.

At age 11, Mario went to **Switzerland** to study. Unfortunately, the students there weren't interested in chemistry either. The same was true when he returned two years later to attend school, and then college, in **Mexico City**.

Finally, at age 25, Molina found people who were as excited about chemistry as he was. It was at the **University of California at Berkeley**, where he studied to get his **Ph.D.** (the highest college degree).

After graduating, Molina started doing research with **Professor F. Sherwood Rowland**. Molina was particularly interested in the gases that were used in **aerosol spray cans, air conditioners**, and **refrigerators**. They're called **CFCs**, short for **chlorofluorocarbons**. He discovered that when CFCs got into the air, they floated high up and ate away at the **ozone layer**. That's a layer of oxygen that protects Earth from the Sun's harmful **ultraviolet rays**.

In **1975**, Molina and other scientists worked hard to inform people about CFCs. They made a bit of progress. But people didn't really pay attention until 1985, when a **big hole** was found in the **ozone layer**! Two years later, many countries signed the **Montreal Protocol** to control the use of CFCs. It's been one of the most successful **environmental agreements** ever. But there's still lots more to do, and scientists are always looking for other ways to clean up the atmosphere.

The letters in MARIO MOLINA can be rearranged to spell MOON AIRMAIL.

iPuzzle
Chemical Symbols

We've listed 14 chemical symbols. Each symbol will be used
once to complete a word below. Use the clues to help you.

silver	argon	gold	chlorine	copper	iron	helium	krypton	lithium	neon	osmium	lead	platinum	xenon
Ag	Ar	Au	Cl	Cu	Fe	He	Kr	Li	Ne	Os	Pb	Pt	Xe

1. University instructor: P R O __Fe__ S S O R

2. Tiny dot on a computer screen: P I ____ L

3. The reason something happens: C ____ S E

4. Bone of an ancient creature: F ____ S I L

5. Scientific study of sight and light: O ____ I C S

6. Idea supported by repeated testing: T ____ O R Y

7. Cells grown in a science experiment: ____ L T U R E

8. Electrons revolve around it: N U ____ E U S

9. Place where things are made: W O R ____ O O M

How many can you get on the first pass?

EXTRA CREDIT

Two different chemical
symbols are needed
for this one ⟶ **10.** An attractive object: M ____ ____ T

⟶ **11.** Paper holder found in many labs: C ____ ____ O ____ D

This one needs three different chemical symbols!

Who Is It? Find a periodic table and look up the chemical
symbols for the elements below. Write them in order in the blanks:
Aluminum + boron + erbium + tellurium + indium + sulfur
+ tellurium + indium = __Al__ ____ ____ ____ ____ ____ ____

Year: 1998 Page: 86

Jump to this
page **or** follow
the pipes.

Molina donated $200,000 (2/3 of his Nobel Prize money) to train students doing environmental research in poorer countries.

1550

Say SVOOL* to **Gerolamo Cardano**, an **Italian mathematician** who invented a way to write **secret messages**. It's called…

The Grille Code

Codes are everywhere. **Computer software** is written in code. People have codes for **security alarms** in their homes. Even this article is written in code (words are code for things, actions, etc.). But best of all are **secret codes** with hidden messages. That's the stuff of spies and soldiers and kids passing notes in the classroom … when their cellphones have been taken away. :-)

A	B	C	D	E	F	G	H	I	J	K	L	M	N	O	P	Q	R	S	T	U	V	W	X	Y	Z
Z	Y	X	W	V	U	T	S	R	Q	P	O	N	M	L	K	J	I	H	G	F	E	D	C	B	A

One of the earliest secret methods was a **substitution code**, where one letter stands for another. In the code above, the **alphabet** is reversed in the bottom row. To encode a message, instead of writing the letter in the top row, the letter just below it is used. So an A would be written using a Z, and the word **CODE** would be written **XLWV**. *Now you can figure out what **SVOOL** means.

Cardano's grille code required two sheets of paper. The first had a note on it anyone could read. The second was a **grille** with holes punched in it. When the grille was placed over the note, the holes would reveal a secret message.

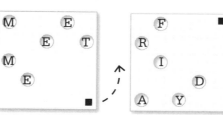

A trickier version, called a **turning grille**, was invented by **Edouard Fleissner von Wostrowitz** in 1880. A secret message is hidden in a **grid** of letters. Placing the grille over the grid reveals the beginning of the message. The rest of the message is revealed by **rotating** the grille once, twice, or three times.

The process of coding or decoding messages is called cryptography.

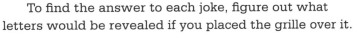

iPuzzle
Grille Jokes

To find the answer to each joke, figure out what
letters would be revealed if you placed the grille over it.

1. What has a bottom at the top?

Y B O G U R F L E S G S

2. Why did the skeleton run away from a fight?

M N O F G K U A T I G S

3. What do you get if you eat onions and baked beans?

T L E J A R F G X H A S

4. If shoes are made from crocodiles, what are made from bananas?

R S O L I U P P E V R S

5. What noise is made when a haunted house is blown up?

A B A N M G A B E O Z O

6. What do you call a dog that loves going for a drive?

P M C A O R L P Y D E T

7. What did Geronimo say when he jumped from an airplane?

X C A M I N H U E K G F

8. If two's company and three's a crowd, what are four and five?

M U N B I P K N C W E O

Grille Puzzle: In 2010, puzzlemaker Mike Nothnagel
and editor Will Shortz presented a grille code crossword puzzle
in *The New York Times*. There was a secret message hiding in
the Friday, Nov. 5 puzzle. But it required using a grille from the
previous day's puzzle (the word HOLE appeared nine times in
the grid). The 9-hole grille revealed the phrase GOLF ROUND.

Jump to this
page **or** follow
the pipes.

1989

Quick, what was the **best-selling toy** in 1991 and 1992? No complaining if you weren't born yet! It was the ...

Super Soaker

splutz

Lonnie Johnson, the inventor of the Super Soaker, was a tinkerer from early on. But it didn't always turn out so well. At age 13, he attached a lawn mower engine to a **go-kart** made from scrap metal and raced it along the highway. The police had to pull him over. A few years later, he burned down part of the kitchen in his house trying to make **rocket fuel**. Rocket fuel!

Nicknamed "**The Professor**" in high school, Lonnie had better luck when he entered the **Alabama state science fair**. A robot made from spare parts and powered by compressed air won him the $250 first prize.

A few years after getting his master's degree in **nuclear engineering**, Johnson took a job with **NASA**. An early project he worked on was creating a nuclear-powered battery for the **Galileo** probe that orbited **Jupiter**. It couldn't use **solar power** because the Sun would be too far away (more than 450 million miles or over 700 million km).

In 1982, while working on a water-powered **heat pump**, Johnson got the idea for the Super Soaker. He attached the heat pump to his bathroom sink one night, to test it. The pump started shooting a powerful stream of water across the room. *This would make a great water gun!* he thought. His 6-year-old daughter agreed.

It took Johnson seven years to perfect his high-powered water gun—and to find a company to make it. It all came together in 1989 when he showed up at the **Larami** toy company in **Philadelphia**. He clicked open a pink beaten-up suitcase and pulled out a sample gun made with white tubing and a plastic soda bottle. It wasn't very impressive, but when it shot a stream of water across the room, knocking coffee cups off a table, the Larami executives were sold!

With the help of a company engineer, the design was simplified so it could be sold for $10. The **water toy** was in stores by the end of the year and was an immediate hit.

More than 300 million Super Soakers were sold in the first 14 years.

Dead end.

The Super Soaker was first sold as the Power Drencher. But that name belonged to another company, so it was changed.

iPuzzle
Super-Duper Squirter

Straight from the iFlush Lab, here's our deluxe squirt gun. Following the tubes from bottle to bottle, find the one way from START to END.

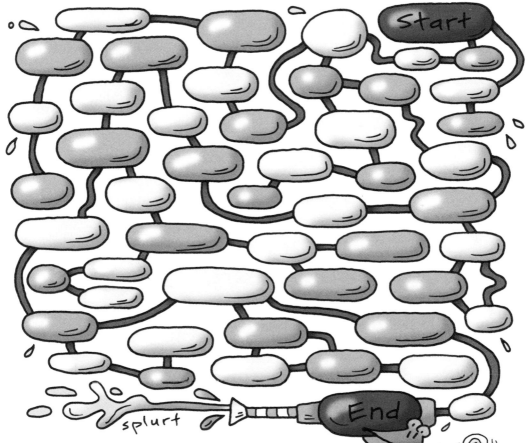

Start

End

splurt

The Winner: One year, the Larami toy company held a contest. New Super Soakers would be given to those with the best reasons for owning one. One winner was a man who was recovering from a heart attack. He said he used a Super Soaker to chase squirrels away from the bird feeder in his yard.

Year:
1992
Page:
38
Go Return

Jump to this page **or** follow the pipes.

1093

I've sloshed my way into the garden estate of **Shen Kuo** in **China**. He's written a book of more than 600 **essays** about...well, everything—science, art, history, even a **toilet goddess** named **Purple Aunty**!

Brush Talks

Shen Kuo's early education came in two forms: 1) reading books under his mother's watchful eye and 2) seeing firsthand how things got done by his father, who was a government official.

Shen grew up to become a high-ranking **government official** himself. He was successful in every role he took on: engineer, financial expert, military leader, manager, inventor, map maker, diplomat, and **imperial academician** (official smart guy). In his spare time, he'd hang out at the **Imperial Palace library** studying math and astronomy. That's right, those were his hobbies!

At age 58, Shen retired to his **garden estate**. He called it **Dream Brook** because it matched a beautiful place he'd repeatedly seen in his dreams. Keeping to himself, Shen set to work writing a book of observations and thoughts. "I had only my writing brush and ink slab to converse with," said Shen. So he titled the book *Brush Talks from Dream Brook*.

About a third of *Brush Talks* was **science**—biology, geography, physics, medicine, geology, archaeology, chemistry, astronomy, meteorology, and mechanics. But there was lots more, including stories.

One entry was titled *Purple Aunty Goes Down to the Mortal World*. It described the custom of inviting the toilet goddess, Purple Aunty, into one's home on the eve of the **Lantern Festival** (the final day of Chinese New Year celebrations). Purple Aunty had the power to turn people into writers and poets.

Shen's book also included some remarkable firsts. His discussion of **compasses** noted that magnetized needles pointed to a spot that wasn't the exact **North Pole**. He also described a printing method using **movable type** (clay blocks, each with a different Chinese character, that could be reused and rearranged). **Europeans** are often credited with both of those discoveries (400 years later!).

iPuzzle
Character Study

Find nine Chinese characters that appear twice and one character that appears three times. Items in black are punctuation and don't count.

中國衣冠，自北齊以來，
乃全用胡服。 ← period

↑ comma

comma used for lists ↓

窄袖、緋綠短衣、長鞾
靴、有鞢帶，皆胡服也。

窄袖利於馳射，短衣、
長鞾皆便於涉草。

this means clothing

The writing above is from Shen's essay on Chinese clothing.

It tells of the short robes, tall boots, and belt ornaments that were common.

UFO? One *Brush Talks* chapter was titled *Strange Happenings*. It told of a huge clam with a pearl in it that repeatedly visited the lakes of Yangzhou. One night, a witness said, it appeared "floating on the water" and "a beam of light penetrated from the shells." The glow was "as white as silver and the pearl was as large as a fist." It then "ran away as quickly as if it were flying."

Year: 1550
Page: 68
Go Return

Jump to this page **or** follow the pipes.

Shen wrote that fossils could be used to explain climate change and land erosion.

1947 **Bell Labs** has just invented the **transistor**, a world-changing device using **quantum mechanics**. What is quantum mechanics? I can't believe I'm saying this, but I'll explain that below!

Weird Science

Don't be scared off by the term quantum mechanics. A **quantum** is the tiniest bit of energy inside an **atom**. And mechanics is the study of motion. So quantum mechanics is the field of science that deals with the motion of tiny stuff inside atoms. And, boy, is that world a weird one!

Take an **electron**, for example. It's a tiny particle that orbits an atom's **nucleus**. Kind of like a planet orbiting the Sun, right? Wrong! Experiments have shown electrons can behave like **waves.** And trying to predict where one will be at any moment is a guessing game because electrons can instantly jump from one orbit to another—making **quantum leaps**!

electron

nucleus

classic drawing of an atom

But it gets even weirder. Two **quanta** (the plural of quantum) can share a mysterious link, even if they're far apart. In one experiment in 2012, scientists took a connected pair of **photons** (quanta of light) and separated them. **Photon 1** was then altered, and guess what? **Photon 2**, on an island 88 miles away (143 km), was instantly altered as well! The two were **entangled**, a strange connection between quanta that no one can really explain.

In fact, there's a lot about quantum mechanics that scientists have trouble explaining. Even **Richard Feynman**, a quantum brainiac, once said, "I think it is safe to say that no one understands quantum mechanics." But here's the thing: quantum mechanics isn't just weird. It's useful! Especially to inventors.

The **transistor** was one of the first inventions using quantum mechanics. It replaced **vacuum tubes**, which were big, easy to break, and needed a lot of electricity. Transistors made the **computers** of today possible. They're also responsible for **digital cameras**, **CD** and **DVD players**, **cell phones**, **ATMs**, **lasers**, and the list goes on and on.

vacuum tube

So, now you know what I know—which isn't much. But hopefully it's more than you knew about quantum mechanics when you woke up today. :-)

Albert Einstein called the idea of entangled quanta "spooky action." And he kept trying to prove it wasn't possible!

iPuzzle
Entanglement

Start at A. From there, either jump from small B to big B (an entangled pair) or from small C to big C (another entangled pair). After each jump, you'll have two new choices. Find the one route that goes from A to M.

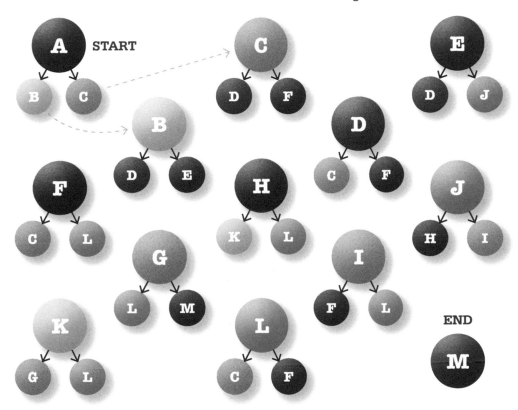

The goal of this puzzle is to get from A to M. (A to M... Hey! That spells ATOM.)

Alternate Universes: One of the most bizarre ideas suggested by quantum mechanics is that every action you take has the potential for a different outcome, each playing out in a different universe. Not all scientists believe this, but the math suggests it's possible. If so, you'll continue reading this book in this universe. But in another, you've just tossed it aside and are eating a big plate of asparagus.

Year: 1949
Page: 54

Jump to this page **or** follow the pipes.

1875

I've come aboard the **HMS** *Challenger*, which has just visited the **hardest-to-reach spot** on the planet!

Challenger Deep

In 1872, a converted British **warship** named HMS *Challenger* began a dangerous journey to explore the world's **oceans**. Six scientists and a crew of over 200 spent three and a half years visiting locations where **oceanographers** (ocean scientists) had never ventured.

The most remarkable place they explored was the **Mariana Trench** near the **Philippines**— the deepest **underwater spot** on earth. It's a world of total darkness farther below the ocean's surface than **Mount Everest** is above it.

Challenger's crew had no way to dive down to the Mariana Trench. The **water pressure** at that depth (the weight of the water pushing down from above) is equal to 10 **Statues of Liberty** stacked one atop the other. Also, the water temperature was barely above freezing. But the scientists had another way of visiting the trench. The crew lowered a long **steel cable** over the side to find the **bottom**. The cable sank...and sank … and sank for an *hour* before hitting the ocean floor at 5.2 miles (8.3 km). That spot was named the **Challenger Deep**.

In 1960, two men visited the Challenger Deep in person. They went in a specially designed sub named *Trieste*, munching chocolate bars on the way down. What they saw at the bottom was a mostly empty landscape of **ooze**, but, to their amazement, they saw a foot-long fish at the bottom staring back at them. The fish then swam slowly into the darkness.

Unmanned vessels followed later and didn't find any fish. But **anemones**, **sea cucumbers**, **jellyfish**, **worms**, and shrimplike creatures called **amphipods** were spotted. Soil samples were scooped up, revealing a thriving world of **amoebas** (single-celled organisms) living under the ocean floor.

In 1995, the Challenger Deep was more accurately measured at 6.8 miles (10.9 km)!

iPuzzle
Challenger Challenge

J.J. Wild, an illustrator aboard *Challenger*, painted this scene at a stop in Fiji. Can you find 5 differences between the original (top) and our version below?

Life On Board: *Challenger* had its own band to provide music. It also had a small population of pets. Among the animals were ostriches, tortoises, and Robert, a parrot who was fond of saying, "What? Two thousand fathoms and no bottom!"

Jump to this page **or** follow the pipes.

The Challenger Expedition cost more than $15 million in 2013 dollars.

In 2012, *Avatar* director James Cameron visited the Challenger Deep in a one-man sub.

J.J. Wild's illustration (above) appeared in his book, *At Anchor*, published in 1878.

1634 We're in **Germany**, where **Johannes Kepler's** book *Somnium* has just been published. Some people call it the world's first work of science fiction.

Sci-Fi

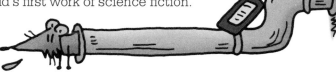

What is **science fiction**? There are different opinions. I like to think of sci-fi as a story that includes scientific stuff, some made up, some not. Marshmallow men living in whipped cream swamps—that's just fantasy. Marshmallow men with **faster-than-light ships** powered by **swamp gas**! That's science fiction.

The ideas in Kepler's *Somnium* first appeared in a paper he wrote as an **astronomy** student. He described what a man would see from the surface of the **Moon**. Just one problem. Kepler described **Earth** as revolving around the **Sun**. Back then, most people thought just the opposite! They believed the Sun and planets all circled Earth. His paper was rejected by his teachers.

Sixteen years later, Kepler decided to rewrite his college paper as a story, thinking it might go over better that way. His story took place in a **dream**, so he titled it *Somnium*. That's Latin for "dream."

In the story, a man is shot to the moon with the help of his mother and a **magical spirit**. Unfortunately, some people thought Kepler based the witchlike mother in the story on his own mother. She was arrested, and *Somnium* was used as evidence at her **witch trial**. If found guilty, she'd be burned at the stake!

It took Kepler over a year to get his mother released. But that didn't stop him from working more on *Somnium*. He added 223 **footnotes** that explained the science behind the story. Those took up more room in the book than the story itself! Four years after his death, the final version of *Somnium* was published.

Moon Men

 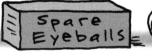

Somnium wasn't the first story to visit the moon. In the second century, a Greek writer named Lucian wrote a novel called *True History*. The tale follows a boatful of men who are carried to the Moon by a tornado. And what a place it is! People wear clothes of glass, and honey runs from their noses. They can take their eyes out, borrowing other people's if theirs get lost. Dog-faced soldiers fly on winged acorns, while other troops use mushroom shields and spears made of ... asparagus!

Kepler is considered one of the great scientists of his time.

The first science fiction magazine, *Amazing Stories*, was started in 1926.

iPuzzle
Lift-off!

Woman in the Moon, a 1929 silent movie, included the world's first rocket-launch countdown. Six cards were shown, reading: 5 seconds, 4, 3, 2, 1…and then what? Use the checklist to eliminate cards, until the correct one remains.

· checklist ·

1. It's a word.

2. It's one word.

3. It has an "O" in it.

4. It has fewer than 3 vowels.

5. It's letters are in alphabetical order.

6. It has an exclamation point.

7. It's not a word on a Monopoly board.

8. It doesn't mean "stop."

BLAST OFF!	**GO!**	**0!**
OOPS	**NOW!**	**IGNITION!**
POWER!	**FIRE!**	**ABORT!**

Sci-fi Greats: In the late 1800s, France's Jules Verne and England's H.G. Wells became the first writers to regularly write science fiction. Because of that, each has been called "The Father of Science Fiction." Robert Goddard, creator of the world's first liquid-cooled rocket, has said he was inspired by Verne's *The Earth to the Moon* and Wells' *War of the Worlds*.

Jump to this page **or** follow the pipes.

1931

Over the years, tons of **ideas** have been passed off as **science**. My favorites are **phrenology**, the study of bumps on the skull, and the **psycograph**, a contraption to measure those bumps.

Quackery...Mostly

Henry Lavery invented the **psycograph**. He and a partner built 33 of the devices and then rented them out to places such as **movie theaters** and **department stores**. Psycographs were good for business—people lined up to have their heads examined!

A psycograph operator would lower a **metal helmet** over a customer's head. The basket-like dome looked like a cross between something in **Dr. Frankenstein's laboratory** and one of those **hair dryers** women sit under in a **beauty salon**. A machine then activated a series of probes that measured **32 spots** on the skull.

Each of those spots was the supposed location of a different **brain organ** just under the surface. **Phrenology experts** believed these organs controlled things such as memory, friendliness, or even hunger. Large organs created **bumps** on the outside of the skull, so they claimed. Small organs created **dents** instead.

After the psycograph measured a person's bumps and dents, the machine printed out a **paper tape**. The printout listed scores for each of the 32 spots. A score of 1 meant deficient. A score of 5? Very superior! The operator could then determine from a chart whether the customer was better suited to being a radio announcer, boxer, farmer, or **genius** (would a genius really be doing this?).

Of course, psycograph readings were complete baloney! You can't tell anything from reading the bumps on people's skulls...well, aside from how bumpy their skulls are. :-)

But here's an odd twist—the idea behind the machine wasn't totally wrong. Brain experts have discovered there are specific **locations inside the brain** that control how we behave and perform activities. You smell food in one part of your brain, tell your arm to push away a plate of **asparagus** in another, and figure out how to get more dessert in still another. But, just to be clear, none of these areas of the brain create bumps or dents on the outside of your head!

Concepts that sound like science, but aren't, are called PSEUDOSCIENCE.

A psycograph shop outside the 1933-1934 Chicago World's Fair was a popular attraction.

iPuzzle
One Lump or Two

Match the correct definition with each brain organ word.
If you need help, the position of the underlined letter in each word
(counting from left to right) matches the number of its definition.

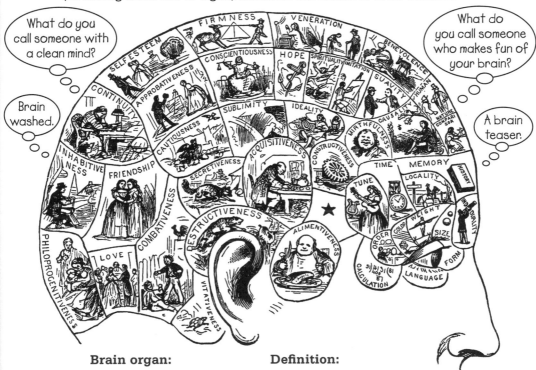

What do you call someone with a clean mind?

Brain washed.

What do you call someone who makes fun of your brain?

A brain teaser.

Brain organ:

A. ___ INHABI<u>T</u>IVENESS
B. ___ VENE<u>R</u>ATION
C. ___ MIRTHFU<u>L</u>NESS
D. ___ APPROBA<u>T</u>IVENESS
E. ___ ALIMENTI<u>V</u>ENESS
F. ___ CAUS<u>A</u>LITY
G. _1_ ⓑENEVOLENCE
H. ___ C<u>O</u>NTINUITY
I. ___ SU<u>A</u>VITY
J. ___ VITAT<u>I</u>VENESS

Definition:

①. kindness
2. ability to focus
3. ability to make friends
4. respect for authority
5. ability to think logically
6. love of life
7. love of home
8. ability to joke around
9. love of being praised
10. enjoyment of food

Year: 1939
Page: 20

Jump to this page **or** follow the pipes.

The above diagram is from *People's Cyclopedia of Universal Knowledge*, published in 1883.

1906 I've "piped" myself to **Bombay, India** (now Mumbai). It's the home of a 10-year-old boy named **Sálim Ali**. In later years, he will become known as…

The Birdman of India

Today, Sálim shot a **sparrow.** :-(Normally, I wouldn't mention such a thing, being a fellow critter. But this loss of one of our chirping chums was different. Sálim had never seen such a bird before. It had a yellow patch on its chest, and he was curious about it. His uncle couldn't identify the bird either, so he sent Sálim to the **Bombay Natural History Society** to find out what it was.

Inside the society's building, Sálim saw seashells, butterflies, and birds' eggs. Mounted **tiger** heads hung on the walls, and stuffed **crocodiles** lay on the floor. When the man in charge saw what Sálim had in his hand, he told him it was a **yellow-throated sparrow**. He then showed Sálim around, telling him about the different birds that lived in India. That moment changed Sálim's life. He left with an armful of books the man had given him and a newfound love of birds.

Sálim Ali's journey to becoming a **bird expert** took a long time. He was a **tungsten miner** for seven years and a **museum guide** and **lecturer** for two. He also spent three years studying **zoology** (animals) and **ornithology** (birds). But in 1930, Ali was without a job. So he invented one!

Ali made a proposal to seven of **India's states** that he perform a study of the birds within their borders. Little was known of them. He asked for no pay, only that his expenses be taken care of. With a budget of 3,000 rupees ($55!) for three months work, he had himself a deal. This was Ali's dream job, roaming the hills and jungles in search of birds.

Ali did a good job, which didn't go unnoticed. More bird work followed. Over the years, Ali visited almost every part of India. He also traveled to places such as **Afghanistan** and the mountains of **Tibet** and **Bhutan**. The knowledge he collected filled many books, giving the people of India and nearby countries a better understanding of the birds with which they shared their lands.

Sálim Ali died in 1987 at the age of 90, recognized as India's great bird expert.

Sálim Ali lost his father and mother by the age of three and was raised by his aunt and uncle.

iPuzzle
Bird Is the Word

Sandwiching Sálim Ali's *last* name between two
letters (an S and an M) turns it into his *first* name!

Create a word in the right column below by adding the correct letter pair
to the front and back. Match up the clues as well (listed in random order).

Clues:	Letter pairs:	Bird names:
1. _B_ it's also a flying toy	C, E	**A.** ___ A W ___
2. ___ baby-delivering bird	H, K	**B.** _K_ I T _E_
3. ___ it's also a rugmaker	~~K, E~~	**C.** ___ O B I ___
4. ___ it lays light blue eggs	R, N	**D.** ___ R A N ___
5. ___ bird of prey	S, K	**E.** ___ T O R ___
6. ___ long-legged wader	W, R	**F.** ___ E A V E ___

. . . .

Clues:	Letter pairs:	Bird-related:
7. ___ fly without flapping	C, K	**G.** _W_ I N _G_
8. ___ hen and rooster's baby	C, N	**H.** ___ O N ___
9. ___ crest on a bird's head	F, L	**I.** ___ O W ___
10. ___ series of bird whistles	G, E	**J.** ___ H I C ___
11. ___ chicken or turkey	S, G	**K.** ___ H I T ___
12. ___ chirp	T, T	**L.** ___ L I D ___
13. _G_ bird's flapper	W, E	**M.** ___ R O W ___
14. ___ color of a swan	~~W, G~~	**N.** ___ W E E ___

Lives Lost: To study birds, Sálim Ali sometimes had to
kill them. He found it necessary for his scientific studies (so did
John James Audubon, America's famous bird expert). But that
doesn't mean Ali approved of killing birds for no reason. He once
said, "It is true that I despise purposeless killing, and regard it
as an act of vandalism, deserving the severest condemnation."

Jump to this
page **or** follow
the pipes.

Words in the puzzle: An OBI is a Japanese sash and a TOR is a rocky hill.

1894

Percival Lowell, a rich guy who was nuts about **astronomy**, has just finished building the **Lowell Observatory** in **Arizona**.

Search for Planet X

Lowell built the observatory hoping its telescopes would prove his claim that **aliens** were building **canals** on **Mars**. Seriously! But when no Martian construction projects could be found, he shifted to searching for a ninth planet in the **Solar System**, one just beyond **Neptune**. He called it **Planet X**.

Lowell died in 1916 without finding Planet X. But the search continued, and on February 18, 1930, another astronomer at the observatory, **Clyde Tombaugh**, did find it. The funny thing is, Lowell had actually photographed Planet X in 1915. He just didn't realize it—the planet appeared as a tiny speck in his photo, and he was looking for something much bigger. :-(

After Planet X's discovery, the big question became what to name it. The answer came from an unexpected source—**Venetia Burney**, an 11-year-old girl from **England**. Her family was talking about the planet's **discovery** one morning at breakfast, and she said, "Why not call it **Pluto**?" Her grandfather liked that, so he passed the name on to an astronomer friend of his who passed it on to the people at Lowell Observatory (the discoverer of a planet gets to name it).

Venetia's suggestion was good for two reasons: 1) Pluto was a **Roman god**, which fit the tradition of naming planets after Greek and Roman gods; and 2) the first two letters were **P-L**, which were Percival Lowell's initials!

On May 1, 1930, Lowell Observatory's director announced Planet X's official name as Pluto. And not long after that, Venetia Burney got a five-pound reward (about $300 today!) from her proud grandfather.

– – – – – – – – – –

Pluto's Demotion :-(

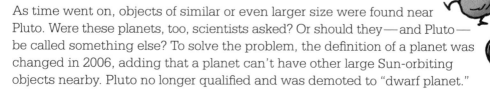

As time went on, objects of similar or even larger size were found near Pluto. Were these planets, too, scientists asked? Or should they—and Pluto—be called something else? To solve the problem, the definition of a planet was changed in 2006, adding that a planet can't have other large Sun-orbiting objects nearby. Pluto no longer qualified and was demoted to "dwarf planet."

The only planet in the Solar System NOT named after a Greek or Roman god is Earth.

iPuzzle
exPLoring

Search for words reading forward, backward, up, down, and diagonally.

PLACEMAT
PLANET
PLANKTON
PLANTATION
PLASTIC
PLATINUM
PLATYPUS
PLAYOFF
PLENTY
PLIERS
PLOW
PLUCK
PLUMBER
PLUNGE
PLURAL
PLUS
PLYWOOD

```
P L A N K T O N L W P J
Q G V O P L U C K O L Y
P I M I T K P L T L A T
V L A T C U B R A P T N
D E A A S I B U M S Y E
O G P T S R T B E U P L
O N L N I A E S C L U P
W U U A N T I A P S L
Y L M L T R U Y L L Z A
L P B P F V O M P P P N
P A E Z H F L Z B T O E
Q A R A F P L U R A L T
```

When has a moon had enough to eat?

When it's full.

What do planets like to read?

Comet books.

Pluto the Pup: One year after the planet Pluto was named, Walt Disney released an animated cartoon titled *The Moose Hunt*. It featured Mickey Mouse and his new pet dog… Pluto! Despite the timing, Walt Disney never admitted that the dog was named after the planet.

Jump to this page **or** follow the pipes.

Lowell Observatory sits on a spot named Mars Hill.

1998 I'm in a **cave** in **Tabasco, Mexico. Sulfuric acid snottites** (gooey drippings that look like something from a runny nose) hang from its roof. The source of this milky white goop? **Bacteria colonies** that snack on sulfur.

Extremophiles!

Extremophile means "extreme lover." That's what scientists call all the weird **life-forms** that love **extreme environments**— places that are freezing, burning hot, pitch black, and so on. Here are some of the oddest extremophiles around.

No light: **Texas blind salamanders** live in water-filled **underground caves** in central Texas. These lizardlike **amphibians** spend their entire lives in total darkness. But that's fine with them because they have no eyes!

Acid: The steaming water in Yellowstone Park's **Lemonade Creek** is bright green from **cyanidium**, an alga that feasts on **arsenic**.

No oxygen: The mud at the bottom of the **Mediterranean Sea** is home to tiny jellyfish-like **brush-heads** that have no need for oxygen.

High heat: Cracks in the ocean floor a mile down spew out seawater heated to 750° F (400° C) by **molten rock**. It's also filled with **dissolved metals** that would kill most life. But six-foot-long **tubeworms** love this scalding mineral bath.

Cold: Wingless **ice bugs** live on mountains, near glaciers, and in ice caves where the temperature is close to **freezing**. If it gets much warmer, they die.

Radioactivity: After the **Chernobyl Nuclear Power Plant** melted down in **Ukraine** in 1986, **black fungi** started growing in the plant and all around it.

Multiple extremes! Tiny 8-legged animals called **water bears** are the extremophile champs. They can survive temperatures as high as 303° F (151° C) and as low as -457° F (-272° C). They can live without water for 10 years and have even survived in **space**. In 2007, they orbited Earth for 10 days— with no water or oxygen, in extreme cold, and exposed to high radiation—and made it back to Earth alive!

Scientists have experimented with oil-eating bacteria that can be used to clean up oil spills.

iPuzzle
Ooh!doku

water bear

ice bug

black fungus

blind salamander

Draw in the missing extremophiles following the rules in the example.

All 4 extremophiles in each column ⟶

All 4 ⟶ extremophiles in each row

All 4 ⟶ extremophiles in each bold box

1.

2.

3.

Alien Life: NASA (National Aeronautics and Space Administration) has been particularly interested in studying extremophiles. Knowing more about the kinds of life that exist on Earth shows the potential for life on other planets or moons—no matter how extreme the environment.

Jump to this page **or** follow the pipes.

The End

The End seemed like a good phrase to use at the end of a book about **toilets**. So that's what I did. Which puts the rest of the book **behind** us. **Butt** you knew that.

I hope you had fun.

I'd hate to think I spent so much time swirling through sewer pipes for nothing! If, for some reason, you didn't have fun (maybe you're one of those **anti-science**, **anti-fun**, **asparagus-eating** kinda people) . . . well, just pretend that you did. For my sake.

Before we leave...

I want to see if you've been paying attention. I mean, there's a ton of stuff to remember from this journey. And nobody can remember all of it, except maybe **Daniel Tammet** and **Kim Peek** (do you remember who they are?).

So let's just see how well you do on this last puzzle the Four P's have posted on the next page. Every question deals with something that appeared in this book.

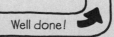
Well done!

iPuzzle
Final Quiz

1. What was the Turtle sub?
   a. ___ a long sandwich served with a bowl of Turtle soup
   b. ___ a tortoise that came off the bench to replace the Turtle
   c. ___ an underwater ship used during the American Revolution

2. Which definition best fits "quantum mechanics"?
   a. ___ car repair guys who fix quantums
   b. ___ a phrase scientists use to scare and confuse people
   c. ___ the study of tiny stuff inside atoms

3. What was Gregor Mendel's middle name?
   a. ___ Legume
   b. ___ Goober
   c. ___ No fair, it was never mentioned!

4. Which word isn't an anagram of TESLA?
   a. ___ stale
   b. ___ least
   c. ___ qualtagh*

5. What is this book's least favorite vegetable?
   a. ___ ketchup
   b. ___ Mr. Potato Head
   c. ___ asparagus

6. Which of these suffer from mytacism (excessive use of M's)?
   a. ___ mammoth
   b. ___ ammonium
   c. ___ Mario Molina
   d. ___ none of the above — every M is necessary

7. Who is the first person you're going to run to tell about this book?
   a. ___ your best friend
   b. ___ your archenemy
   c. ___ a qualtagh*

* *n.* the first person you see when you leave your house (it's a real word!)

Answers

9. Lens Sense

1. SUDDENLY 2. LEMONS 3. LISTEN
4. SPLINTER 5. WRESTLING 6. STOLEN
7. GASOLINE 8. LONGEST 9. ANTLERS

11. Space Zoo Search

13. Tesla: Yes or No?

1. YES 2. NO 3. YES 4. YES
5. NO 6. YES 7. YES 8. YES

15. One-Line Drawings

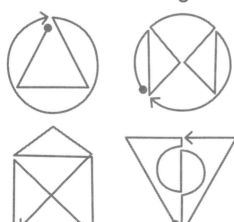

17. Maze Ball

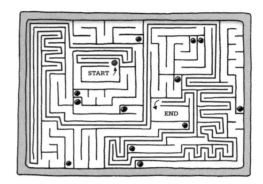

19. Bronze Medal

Put them together in this order, from top
to bottom: 3, 9, 4, 1, 8.

21. Robot Code

HEAVY METAL, HE WAS RUSTY

Extra credit: 9 in binary is 1001.

23. Spud Jokes

1. D 2. I 3. G 4. A 5. H

6. B 7. F 8. C 9. E 10. J

25. On Display

2 and 6 are the fakes.

A . $7 + 1 = 8$ B. $6 - 2 = 4$ C. $1 + 4 = 5$
D. $13 - 12 = 1$ E. $8 - 5 = 3$ F. $4 + 3 = 7$

27. Plastic Surgery

1. HEEL 2. TYPE 3. ONLY

4. PAT 5. LEATHER 6. THE

7. HEALTHY 8. ELEPHANT
9. EEL 10. POTTERY

29. Making a Beeline

31. In Other Words

We found 87 common words:

AIL, AIM, AIR, ALE, ARE, ARM, ART,
ATE, EAR, EAT, ELM, ERA, ETA, IRE,
LAM, LEA, LET, LIE, LIT, MAR, MAT,
MET, MIL, RAM, RAT, RIM, TAR, TEA,
TIE, TIL, EARL, EMIT, ITEM, LAIR,
LAME, LATE, LIAR, LIME, MAIL, MALE,
MALT, MARE, MART, MATE, MEAL,
MEAT, MELT, META, MILE, MIRE, MITE,
RAIL, RATE, REAL, REAM, RIME, RITE,
TAIL, TALE, TAME, TEAL, TEAM, TEAR,
TERM, TIER, TILE, TIME, TIRE, TRAM,
TRIM, ALERT, ALTER, IRATE, LATER,
LITER, MATER, MERIT, METAL, MITER,
REALM, REMIT, TAMER, TIMER, TRAIL,
TRIAL, MAILER, MITRAL, RETAIL.

33. Asteroids

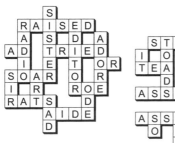

35. Chladni Plates

The plates in the upper right and lower left corners are identical.

37. Energy Anagrams

1. D   2. G   3. A   4. B   5. K   6. H
7. L   8. C   9. E   10. F   11. J   12. I

39. Splash Match

41. Lipstick on the Loose

43. Pick a Lock

Unlocking #2 will separate all the others.

45. Sssnake Sssearch

47. Quinine Nine

1. missing flowers   2. missing leaf
3. angle of stem   4. missing flowers
5. chewed leaf
6. angle of leaf
7, 8, and 9:
missing
leaves

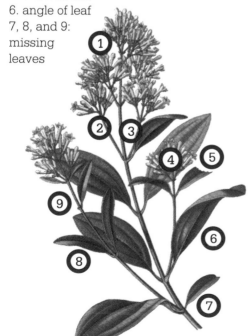

51. The Four Peas

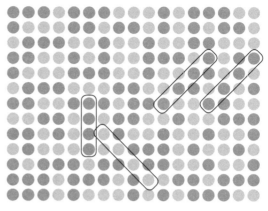

53. Lemon "Juice"

55. Bar Code Jokes

Sitting or standing, hold the page just under your eyes so it's parallel to the ground. The type in the answers will be shortened to reveal the answers below. You'll have to look at the book from different directions to read them all.

1. A - A MEAT BALL
2. C - LEAN BEEF
3. D - PACIFIC OCEAN
4. E - THE LIVING ROOM
5. F - NICE BELT
6. B - USE A RULER

57. Flo's Challenge

Here are 46 words we found:

A, AT, BE,HE, ARE, ART, ATE, BAR,
BAT, BET, BRA, EAR, EAT, ERA, ETA,
HAT, HER, RAT, TAB, TAR, TEA, THE,
ABET, BARE, BATE, BATH, BEAR, BEAT,
BETA, BRAE, BRAT, HARE, HART, HATE,
HEAR, HEAT, HERB, RATE, TARE, TEAR,
BATHE, BERTH, EARTH, HATER, HEART,
BATHER. **Extra credit:** TELEGRAPH

59. What's That Mean?

1. R	2. L	3. M	4. A	5. K
6. F	7. T	8. Q	9. B	10. H
11. C	12. D	13. J	14. O	15. I
16. S	17. P	18. N	19. G	20. E

61. Turtle Doodles

1. F   2. E   3. A   4. C   5. B   6. D

63. Tongue Twisters

1. C	2. J	3. G	4. F	5. I
6. H	7. A	8. E	9. D	10. B

65. Prime Time

The prime numbers are 2, 3, 5, 7, 11, 13,
17, 19, 23, 29, 31, 37, 41, 43, 47, 53, 59, 61,
67, 71, 73, 79, 83, 89, and 97.

67. Chemical Symbols

1. Fe   2. Xe = pixel   3. Au = cause
4. Os = fossil   5. Pt = optics
6. He = theory   7. Cu = culture
8. Cl = nucleus   9. Kr = workroom
10. Ag, Ne = magnet
11. Li, Pb, Ar = clipboard

69. Grille Jokes

1. your legs   2. no guts   3. tear gas
4. slippers   5. bamboo   6. carpet
7. me   8. nine

71. Super-Duper Squirter

73. Character Study

Characters of the same color are matches.

中國衣冠，自北齊以來，
乃全用胡服。

窄袖、緋綠短衣、長鞵靴、
有鞢帶，皆胡服也。

窄袖利於馳射，短衣、
長鞵皆便於涉草。

75. Entanglement

A - B - E - J - H - K - G - M

77. Challenger Challenge

1. tree added
2. tree missing
3. hut missing
4. person missing
5. boat moved to left

79. Lift-off!

NOW!

81. One Lump or Two

A. 7   B. 4   C. 8   D. 9   E. 10
F. 5   G. 1   H. 2   I. 3   J. 6

83. Bird Is the Word

1. B	A. HAWK
2. E	B. KITE
3. F	C. ROBIN
4. C	D. CRANE
5. A	E. STORK
6. D	F. WEAVER
7. L	G. WING
8. J	H. SONG
9. M	I. FOWL
10. H	J. CHICK
11. I	K. WHITE
12. N	L. GLIDE
13. G	M. CROWN
14. K	N. TWEET

85. exPLoring

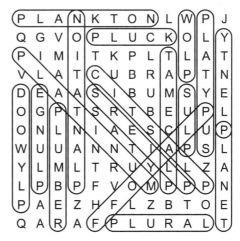

87. Ooh!doku

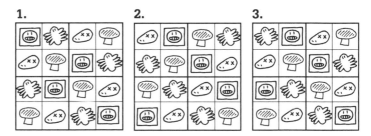

89. Final Quiz

1. c   2. c   3. c   4. c   5. c
6. d (in our opinion)   7. That's up to you!

iBonus
Blow Up This Book!

What's a science book without one last experiment?
Here's a fun one using simple equipment in your home.

1. Supplies

- small plastic bottle
- baking soda
- vinegar
- balloon
- marker pen
- funnel
- large white shirt to wear as your lab coat

2. Make Your Own iFlush Lab

A kitchen, bathroom, or somewhere outside will do the trick.

Pick a spot where spilling isn't a problem.

3. Balloon

Draw a picture of this book on the balloon. Just a rectangle with "iFlush" in it will do.

4. Baking Soda

Use the funnel to put one tablespoon of baking soda in the balloon.

5. Vinegar

Fill the bottle with an inch of vinegar. Use the (cleaned) funnel if necessary.

6. Attach

Stretch the balloon onto the bottle's top. Don't let the baking soda fall into the bottle yet.

7. Combine!

Lift the balloon so the baking soda falls into the vinegar.

8. Expand

Carbon dioxide from the mixture will inflate the balloon.

9. Ta da!

You've **blown up** this book.

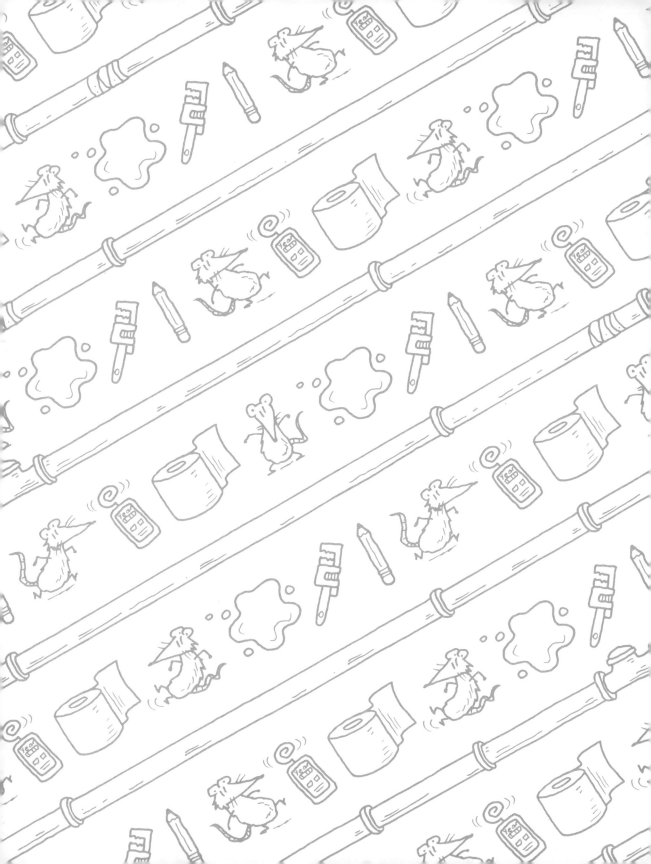